CULTURE AND PERSONALITY

STUDIES IN
Anthropology

Consulting Editors:

MORTON H. FRIED
AND MARVIN HARRIS

Columbia University

CULTURE
AND
PERSONALITY

Anthony F. C. Wallace

University of Pennsylvania

RANDOM HOUSE · NEW YORK

Editor's Foreword

With this work by Anthony F. C. Wallace, we introduce *Studies in Anthropology,* a series of paperbound volumes surveying the fields, subfields, and some major complexes of problems in this rapidly growing discipline.

It is a fortunate coincidence that *Culture and Personality* should appear as the first book in this series. For while Dr. Wallace's subject concerns an area that has for some decades been recognized as *terra anthropoligica,* it at the same time touches on the adjacent physiological and psychological realms of biology. And necessarily so. Anthropology, as the science of culture, cannot properly focus exclusively on man; yet since man is the only real culture carrier that we know, his exclusion from our analyses would make even less sense.

As Wallace and others have pointed out. much of the work in the field of personality and culture is notorious for its imprecision and "softness." The problem of devising and maintaining sharp and useful distinctions between levels of different analytical complex-

28007ᵛ

ity has proven most difficult. We are therefore fortunate in being able to launch the present series with a treatment that fully recognizes such difficulties and that stresses the operational means by which contrasting abstractions may be used to derive new hypotheses and help throw new light on those already at hand.

It is hoped that the high standards of Dr. Wallace's approach will be maintained by the contributors to follow. As is expected of all the titles to come, *Culture and Personality* is not merely a review of basic concepts, a critique of past ventures, and a summary account of some of the latest researches. First and foremost, it is a paper in which its author takes a position. And whether the position taken should anger or please, confuse or clarify, its ultimate purpose is to advance the reader's understanding of the complex problems of this and related branches of human and cultural science.

Each book in this series is intended to stand by itself and can be read individually. Yet in a larger sense, the *Studies in Anthropology* are seen by the editors as comprising an over-all unity, with later titles referring to those already published. On occasion, for example, a problem taken up in one particular context in one study will be treated somewhat differently in another. Thus, Wallace's concern with the evolution of psychological capacities in the Pleistocene will find echoes in three subsequent books—the one to be devoted to the evolution of culture up to the Neolithic, the one on race, and the one discussing the role of evolutionary theory in anthropology. Since each of these will have a different author, they will show how much agreement may be developing with regard to some of the basic issues and concepts of the larger discipline.

For his aid in making this series possible, the editors thank Mr. Charles D. Lieber of Random House.

Morton H. Fried & Marvin Harris

Preface

THIS STUDY IN CULTURE-AND-PERSONALITY expresses the writer's belief that the main business of science is to describe, in sufficiently general language for the descriptions to be valid beyond the individual case, how classes of systems work. In order to carry on this business successfully, the scientist must be constantly skeptical; he must use concepts and techniques of observation which will make possible a demonstration of the predictive value, and not merely the plausibility, of his general assertions. Hence, in this study we shall not attempt to summarize empirical studies of particular peoples, nor to present a comprehensive bibliography of such studies. The emphasis will fall on such logical and methodological foundations as culture-and-personality, as science, may possess, and the bibliography is intended only to refer the reader to representative papers and books useful in discussing these foundations. The student and the instructor should use this brief study in conjunction with a collection of descriptive papers and monographs which will flesh out the skeleton of concepts and generalizations.

Many persons have directly or indirectly contributed to the forming of the writer's approach to culture-and-personality. To Dr. A. Irving Hallowell and Dr. Loren C. Eiseley in particular, acknowledgment is due for encouraging him as a student to work in this area and to extend his methodological and theoretical interests beyond the conventional boundaries of the subject. Other colleagues and friends will recognize, and hopefully will not be distressed by, the uses to which their encouragement and suggestions have been put. To all of them, named and unnamed, the writer is grateful.

Portions of several chapters have been presented in the form of papers read to scientific audiences. The discussion of equivalence structures in Chapter I incorporates much of a paper entitled, "Equivalence Structures and the Cultural Articulation of Private Cognitive Worlds," read at the Cognitive Structures Symposium at the 1959 meetings of the American Anthropological Association in Mexico City. Most of Chapter II is drawn from a paper on evolution and the brain read to the 1958 seminar on the biological foundations of behavior at the Albert Einstein College of Medicine, Yeshiva University, New York.

A.F.C.W.

Contents

TABLES AND FIGURES

[I]

Introduction

IN THIS SHORT STUDY of culture-and-personality, we shall be guided by two assumptions about the field of anthropology itself: first, that it is the business of anthropology to develop a scientific theory of culture; and second, that any theory which pretends to explain, or to predict, cultural phenomena must include in its formulations non-cultural phenomena. Many of these latter non-cultural phenomena can be subsumed under the general rubric of "personality."

THE PURPOSE OF THIS STUDY

IN ORDER TO form a critical synopsis of any special branch of knowledge, the student must state in summary form certain major laws, principles, theories, or substantive discoveries which have current significance in that field of knowledge, and must evaluate the internal logical and methodological structure of the field of knowledge itself. In the former task, the locus of reference is the "real world," the primary reality "out there," of observable phenomena which the scientist is attempting to describe, predict, and understand. In the latter task, the locus of reference is not the primary

1

phenomena, but the scientific process itself by which these phenomena are being studied. It is one of the conspicuous features of modern science that major advances in substantive knowledge depend upon major advances in the self-awareness of the scientist. Only as the scientist comes to recognize and to take account of the limitations imposed on his vision by the concepts he chooses to consider important, and by the assumptions he makes about the logic of inference and the technique of observation, can he achieve the flexibility of approach required to solve new problems.

Particularly in anthropology, among all the social sciences, is the need for self-evaluation now acute. Gamboling in the world-garden of culture, anthropologists have only lately begun to realize that new ethnographic description, like daily weather reporting, is an endless task. There is not a finite number of cultures which, once described, will stay fixed forever on some *scala culturae*. Culture change is constant, ubiquitous, and only moderately predictable; the ethnographic inventory will never be complete and will ever have to be supplemented by ethnographic monitoring. Thus, the problem for the theoretical anthropologist has shifted from the Linnaean classification of cultures and their aspects on a temporal or geographic continuum to the discovery and analysis of the laws of cultural process. These laws, furthermore, are recognized by most investigators to involve the dynamics, not merely of "cultural" entities, but of ecological, demographic, physiological, and psychological entities as well. It is about as meaningful to claim that "culture must be explained in terms of culture," leaving out biological and psychological "levels" of explanation, as to assert that "life must be explained in terms of life," without reference to chemistry and physics.

Culture-and-personality thus is significant in the field of cultural anthropology because it is concerned with certain aspects of the theory of culture process. The kind of process to which it addresses its attention includes the intergenerational transfer of culture ("enculturation" or socialization), culture change, the institutionalization of modes of coping with individual diversity, and the like. It is least significant in cultural monitoring: a good ethnography permits far more accurate prediction of specific behavior than does any national character study. Its *raison d'être* resides in the fact that it systematically takes account of non-cultural data in explaining and predicting cultural phenomena.

But while the strategic importance of culture-and-personality is great, it has not inspired universal confidence among anthropologists. It has to many (including the writer) often seemed to be "soft" in logical structure and in research method. This partial failure to gain acceptance commensurate with its pretensions has been owing to several circumstances. One circumstance has been the insularity of the brand of psychology which it has chiefly utilized, namely, psychoanalytic theory. Despite the claim of Freud, its creator, that psychoanalysis is based on biological knowledge, his disciples have so heavily emphasized the autonomy of psychological process that two-way bridges between dynamic psychology and physiology have been few. This has tended to reduce the natural affinity between culture-and-personality and the relatively "hard" sciences of neurology, general physiology, biochemistry, and experimental psychology. Personality theory, which emphasizes the affects, has also been somewhat insulated from the academic psychological core-tradition and its concern with perceptual, cognitive, and learning processes. A complementary difficulty has been the slowness with which physical anthropology itself (to which anthropologists in search of physiological knowledge might reasonably turn) has taken up the vast resources of the modern sciences of neurology, general physiology, biochemistry, psychopharmacology, and so on. And a final obstacle has been the fact that most of those who have worked in culture-and-personality were trained, as graduate students, to be descriptive ethnographers, with only peripheral acquaintance with the other substantive fields to which we have referred, or with formal logic, mathematics, descriptive statistics, and the like. Thus, even with the best will in the world, culture-and-personality workers have been hampered in their efforts to advance the theoretical understanding of cultural processes by a relative unfamiliarity with some of the necessary tools.

There is evidence that this unsatisfactory situation is improving now. The continuing popularity of interdisciplinary research, despite the common disillusionment which afflicts some of its overly enthusiastic practitioners, attests to the awareness of the need to approach theoretical problems on many "levels" simultaneously. Much of such research has become institutionalized, beyond the project level, in various institutes, research centers, seminars, and combined departmental programs. Participation in such activities has led many anthropologists to extend their training and interest to other fields, and to incorporate into their own thinking the data and concepts of other disciplines. It is to be hoped and expected that eventually this process of ideological expansion will result in culture-and-personality training programs which require the student to take formal instruction in such subjects as physiology, symbolic logic and mathematics, and cognitive theory, as well as in descriptive statistics, dynamic psychology, and projective testing.

The present chapter is concerned with evaluating certain features of culture-and-personality as an intellectual system; the other four chapters of this study will present and appraise some of the salient themes of the descriptive and theoretical literature. Our evaluation of the field will not merely list major interests and then invoke the pious ideal of scientific rigor; we shall be concerned to expose specific contradictions, inadequacies, and flaws, and to point out promising new avenues of attack, in the hope of arousing discussion and, ultimately, progress by interested students. The treatment may seem, in some cases, to be harsh; the intention of criticism, however, is not to destroy but to stimulate further growth, sometimes by pruning.

To help us there is now available a small group of books and articles which make some critical review of the field. Some of these reviews are partisan: Lindesmith and Strauss (1950), for instance, have written a critique of the conceptual and methodological deficiencies of culture-and-personality writings, which should be read carefully by anyone undertaking to do work in this field; in response to what he regards as neglect and as "vulgar" and "irresponsible" distortions of Freud made by anthropologists, LaBarre has penned a vigorous defense of the proposition that "nothing human can escape illumination from the penetrating, pan-human and holistic psychology of Freud" (LaBarre, 1958); Margaret Mead has defended the methodology of national character studies (Mead, 1953); Hsu (1952) has deplored the tendency of anthropologists to accept without hesitation any and all psychiatric generalizations about the relations between child care and adult personality, whether based on empirical evidence or mere "authority"; and Kaplan (1957) has questioned "the broadness of the way the concept of internalization is used"—and thus questioned the main postulate of much of traditional culture-and-personality theory. Other reviewers (Honigmann, 1954; Kluckhohn, 1954; Inkeles, 1954) are less critical, more inclined to describe the varieties of approach which have been used. But there is no need to review the reviews; the student can consult the bibliography appended to this study and then turn to these works directly. We are here concerned with making our own evaluation of the main assumptions of culture-and-personality as a branch of science.

OPERATIONAL DISCRIMINATIONS AMONG CONCEPTS

THE MOST CELEBRATED definition of culture is Tylor's:

> Culture . . . is that complex whole which includes knowledge, belief, art, morals, law, custom, and any other capabilities and habits acquired by man as a member of society.

If the word "personality" is substituted for "culture" in the above sentence and the phrase "the individual" for "man," it will serve as a passable definition of personality as well. But there are, of course, other definitions of varying levels of abstractness, each one emphasizing those dimensions of observation which are most appealing to its author. The writer, for instance, in a probabilistic mood, suggested (1952b) that culture be defined as:

> . . . those ways of behavior or techniques of solving problems which, being more frequently and more closely approximated than other ways, can be said to have a high probability of use by individual members of society.

Personality, in this context, would be simply:

> . . . those ways of behavior or techniques of solving problems which have a high probability of use by one individual.

Usually the author of any such a definition has in mind some kind of observation by which individual cultures or personalities are recognized, bounded, and properly described. The ethnographer may have in mind, when he gives a definition of culture, a long sequence of operations, beginning with learning the language, taking photographs, talking to people, watching what goes on and trying it himself, and fifteen years later ending up with intricate comparative analysis of recorded data by the use of some specific schema, based on a particular theoretical position. An archaeologist has in mind ecological parameters, digging, certain types of durable material remains, classification, labelling, and analysis by an equally specific but different schema. A psychoanalyst, when he thinks of "personality," has in mind the characteristic individual shape of psychodynamic structures whose elements are oedipal conflicts, castration anxieties, imagos, mechanisms of defense, and so forth; while the clinical psychologist, describing personality structure from Rorschach test data, is visualizing a bar graph, based on frequencies of such phenomena as allusions to color, line, texture, perspective, and movement, and is inferring such characteristics as introversion, stereotypy, imaginativeness, and self-control. Thus, there is no one concept of culture, nor a single concept of personality, which is universally agreed upon and is universally useful.

We do not propose to list here a set of definitions of the words "culture" and "personality," and then, by some suitable criteria, to select the best. Nor shall we offer new definitions. The student should realize that dozens, if not hundreds, of respectable definitions exist. Most of them, unfortunately, are ontological definitions: that is to say, they assert that culture *is* such and such, or that personality *is* one thing or another. And ontological definitions are the bane of science. They postulate Platonic essences, states of being in a realm of absolutes, about which argument may rage endlessly without any resolution but that of authority. Discussion of such definitions is sterile, as Hume pointed out long ago, when in his *Enquiry Concerning Human Understanding* (1748, Sect. XII, Part 3) he made the famous assertion:

> If we take in our hand any volume . . . let us ask, *Does it contain any abstract reasoning concerning quantity or number?* No. *Does it contain any experimental reasoning concerning matter of fact and existence?* No. Commit it then to the flames: for it can contain nothing but sophistry and illusion.

The more profitable procedure is to regard the words "culture" and "personality" as the names for indefinitely large numbers of different empirical operations. All of the operations under the rubric "culture" have in common certain broad and general features, and similarly with those referrable to "personality." An examination of textbooks and symposia concerning human personality will reveal, for instance, that a number of theories of personality dynamics and a bewildering variety of observational techniques are employed by dozens of authorities: projective tests, depth interviews, questionnaires, life histories, laboratory experiments, verbalized introspection, and so forth, on an infinitude of subject matters. And on these data various distinctive and stylized abstractive manipulations are performed, the results of which are treated as descriptive of various traits, forces, factors, vectors, structures, and so on, in many different arrangements. Similarly, with materials on culture: in-

formant interviews, participant observation, film strips
and photographs, tape-recorded texts, published literature, censuses, maps, material objects, and so on, are
collected, and then subjected to various abstractive and
analytical procedures, the products whereof are regarded
as constituting an ethnographic description. Obviously,
whatever culture "is" and whatever personality "is," the
empirical operations by which they are described vary,
depending on both the observer and the situation of his
observations.

It is possible, however, to discriminate between these
two words, and others relevant to this area of inquiry,
and to describe their relationship in terms of certain of
their operational characteristics. Three dimensions are
of particular relevance: the number of persons observed,
directly or indirectly; the number of kinds of behavior
observed; and the level of abstraction achieved by various analytic and synthetic operations. All three dimensions of variation, furthermore, are to be considered
under a constant condition; namely, that the observations are made of individuals within the boundaries of
a specified population at a given time. The semantic relationships can best be represented in tabular form. First,
we shall consider only the first two dimensions, of number of individuals and number of behavioral categories
observed, allowing level of abstraction to vary. Table 1 *
represents the operational differentiation of several terms
(some of them to be further defined later in the text) by
number of individuals and by number of behavioral categories.

* This table is an amplification of a smaller schema devised
in manuscript by Mr. Theodore Graves to illustrate the meaning of several socio-psychological terms by reference to the
concepts of behavior potential, expectancy, and reinforcement
value, derived from his work with Dr. Julian Rotter on social
learning. See Rotter, Julian B., *Social Learning and Clinical
Psychology* (Englewood Cliffs, N.J.: Prentice-Hall, 1954).

TABLE 1

CULTURE-AND-PERSONALITY TERMINOLOGY DIFFERENTI-
ATED BY NUMBERS OF INDIVIDUALS AND OF BEHAVIOR
CATEGORIES OBSERVED

1. When one has observed

   one individual in a group,
   many individuals in a group,
   all individuals in a group,

2. and the behavior observed is, in the language of this investigation, of

   one category (i.e., a particular class of act, or sequence
     of acts, consistently performed in a class of situations),
   many categories, arranged in an equivalence structure,
   all those categories which exist in some equivalence struc-
     ture,

3. then, depending on the abstractive operations, the statement
   of the observations will be a description of a . . .

NUMBER OF BEHAVIOR CATEGORIES

	ONE CATEGORY	TWO OR MORE CATEGORIES	ALL CATEGORIES
ONE	habit, response, behavior potential, etc. 1	character trait, motive, complex, value, syndrome, etc. 4	mazeway, personality, psycho-biological system, etc. 7
TWO OR MORE	culture trait, custom, role, alternative, specialty, etc. 2	relationship, institution, ritual, theme, etc. 5	sub-culture, status personality, etc. 8
ALL	culture trait, custom, role, theme, universal, etc. 3	relationship, institution, ritual, theme, focus, etc. 6	pattern, configuration, culture, national character, modal personality, etc. 9

NUMBER OF INDIVIDUALS

The contents of Table 1 (and the meaning of the expression "equivalence structure") can perhaps best be illuminated by a series of nine illustrations, corresponding to the nine cells of the table:

CELL 1. We observe that an old American Indian man, who lives alone in a small house on a reservation where we are staying, whenever he leaves the house (to walk to the general store, or to visit relatives, or for whatever reason) props a stick of wood against the lockless door. On being asked why he does this, he says, "It is a sign to people that I am away and that they should not enter." Without any further information about this type of behavior, we temporarily regard it as a personal *habit*.

CELL 2. On further inquiry, we find that a dozen of our acquaintances on this reservation follow the same practice when they leave the house empty: they prop a stick of wood, or a broom, against the door. They all say, on inquiry, that it is a sign of the occupant's temporary absence and of his wish that no one enter. Some aver that almost everyone on the reservation does this. We conclude that putting a stick against the door is a *custom* in this community, regularly followed by many persons when they leave a dwelling temporarily empty. Comparing notes later with another anthropologist, we learn that the same custom is practiced on a number of reservations in the area, and we begin to refer to it as a *culture trait* with an unknown distribution.

CELL 3. Although we are unable to make inquiry in every household in the community, we are told by some of our informants that almost everyone on the reservation props a stick against the door when leaving the house. We consider that it is likely that this custom is also a cultural *universal* on this reservation, but hesitate to make the claim categorically because of the difficulty and expense of even the attempt to demonstrate universality in the field.

CELL 4. Our curiosity is now piqued. We come from a city in which the custom is to lock all doors and windows when the house is empty and, if the absence is to be lengthy, to leave some sign (such as a burning light or the absence of accumulated mail) that the house is occupied. The rationale usually given for doing this is the prevention of theft and vandalism. We note that the Indian custom draws attention to the owner's absence, rather than conceals it, and that the leaning stick of wood constitutes no barrier to entry, since the door is not locked. Several speculations occur to us: First of all, we feel sure that the absent owner is confident that his neighbors will not enter his house when a stick is propped against the door; in other words, that he conceives of the two types of behavior as being equivalent, and therefore expects that his house will be left alone if he plays the stick-propping role. Secondly, we suspect that any Indian who "stick-props" will probably display certain other behaviors as well, which have in common a quality of confidence that explicit requests will be honored. Our interest in this possibility leads us to go back to our earlier informant, whose habit of stick-propping had first led us to the subject. We interview him at some length, not only on stick-propping, but on matters related to confidence in the granting of wishes, and learn that he does indeed regard personal requests, both to him and from him, as carrying an expectation of fulfillment. He makes requests of us, once we get to know him, for transportation, for errands, for legal advice, and for gifts of food, tobacco, and even money. On the other hand, he freely accedes to our wishes that he spend time as an informant without pay, accompanies us in order to introduce us to others, shares his own limited resources without stint. We feel that, at least in contrast to most whites whom we know, he has a characterological *trait* of expectation of wish-granting, whether he be the wisher or the grantor.

CELL 5. Indeed, as we come to know many people on the reservation, we find that this wish-granting expectancy trait is so common that we can call it a *theme* in the culture. We now observe that on several occasions, when we have gone with one or another of our informants to visit a house where someone can give us certain information, our guide will not bother to knock on a door against which a stick is propped, nor will he enter in order to look for or await the occupants. We are told, several times, "You don't go into a house when a stick is propped against the door." We conclude that stick-propping and house-avoidance behaviors constitute, for many pairs of persons, complementary roles; the two behaviors are equivalent in the logician's sense that whenever, but only when, person A plays role a, person B will play role b. We begin to refer to this equivalence structure as an *institution*.

CELL 6. Inasmuch as we suspect, although we cannot demonstrate, that the complementary stick-propping and house-avoidance behaviors are universals, and inasmuch as this institution is only one expression of a more general theme of expectancy of wish-granting, we feel that we may now be dealing with an area of cultural *focus*. This hypothesized focus would fall on the development and maintenance of institutions which express the theme of expectancy of wish-granting. The pursuit of this hypothesis leads us to consider that wishes expressed in dreams are, indeed, historically known to have been the source of a number of cultural innovations, as for instance the cultural reforms sponsored by a religious prophet in the previous century. We observe also that many religio-medical secret societies, and even major political institutions, in myth are asserted to have originated in dreams or dreamlike wishes.

CELL 7. Because we are now on good terms with the old man, we ask him whether he will tell us the story of his life, recount some of his dreams, and be a subject for several tests, including the Rorschach and the TAT. Although he displays some discomfort, particularly about recounting dreams (which we expected), he feels that he must grant our wish. The indelicacy of asking for dreams he excuses on the grounds that we are whites, and white people have different customs; hence, telling us his dreams is "not the same thing" as telling a neighbor. We thus obtain a large body of psychological materials. The product of their analysis we regard as a description of the structure of his *personality,* since the statements made in this description are abstractions which we consider to be relevant to virtually all areas of his behavior.

CELL 9. In addition to working with the old man, we have been obtaining similar, if less extensive, projective test data from a large number of persons on the reservation. Furthermore, we have, with the help of several excellent informants and of our own day-by-day observation, been filling in the content categories of the *Outline of Cultural Materials.* These large bodies of data we do not analyze carefully in the field, but on our return to the University we work with them and produce, from the projective test data, a description of the *modal personality structure* of the population and, from the ethnographic data, a sketch of the *culture.*

CELL 8. One probable source of error in any general attribution to all members of the society of the modal personality description, derived by the procedures outlined for Cell 9, is the existence of sex, age, and other social differentials in the sample. Wishing to avoid the possibility of an unwary reader's attributing the modal personality type to sub-groups where personality norms actually differ significantly from the modal type, we construct separate modal types for males and females, for children, active adults, and inactive ("old") adults, and for the two major ethnic groups which compose the population (approximately one-third of the tribe are sixth-generation immigrant refugees from another culture area). This refinement of the analysis reveals that there are indeed significant differences among the modal types constructed for age, sex, and ethnic sub-groups within the population, and between some of these sub-types and the general type. This discovery of distinctive *status personalities,* which correspond roughly with the *sub-cul-*

tures of distinctive social sub-groups, does not invalidate the modal personality type characteristic of the population as a whole, of course, since its definition involved specification of its relative frequency within the population. But it makes possible much more exact understanding of the interpersonal dynamics of the society than dependence on knowledge of the general modal type would permit.

The careful student will note, in the foregoing illustrations and in Table 1, that there is a certain arbitrariness in the decision to regard the product of some observation as belonging to the first, second, or third column. This arbitrariness is the result of the fact that, although the same category of overt behavior may be described in terms of either culture or personality, what constitutes a single category (or class) of behavior will depend on the concern of the investigator. In one study, a number of things which a mother does, in relation to her offspring, may be classified as one category of behavior and referred to as "mothering" (column 1). In another study, the mother's role may be construed as a large number of more particular behaviors, such as feeding, cleaning, fondling, and so on, each of which is treatable in column 1; in this case, "the mother role" will operationally fall within column 2. This ought not to concern the student, however, since the important thing is not to construct an absolute classification of constructs, but to be able to specify their operational relationship within any given investigation.

Another source of ambiguity is the fact that each cell beyond 1 can contain constructs at varying levels of abstraction from the same body of primary observations. Thus, for example, in Cell 7, *mazeway* refers to the entire set of cognitive maps of positive and negative goals, of self, others, and material objects, and of their possible dynamic interrelations in process, which an individual

maintains at a given time. *Personality* covers the same
territory, but on a higher level of abstraction, in which
mazeway particulars are classified and grouped under
various rubrics, such as the wish-fulfillment trait which
we used in our illustration, a hysterical syndrome, or
whatever. The relations among the constructs in the
third column of Table 1 may be represented by an expansion, as in Table 2 (page 20).

Some further discussion of the concept of mazeway
may be appropriate here. *Mazeway* is to the individual
what *culture* is to the group. Just as every group's history
is unique, so every human individual's course of experience is unique. Every human brain contains, at a given
point of time, as a product of this experience, a unique
mental image of a complex system of objects, dynamically interrelated, which includes the body in which the
brain is housed, various other surrounding things, and
sometimes even the brain itself. This complex mental
image is the mazeway. Its content consists of an extremely large number of assemblages, or cognitive resi-
dues of perception. It is used, by its holder, as a true
and more or less complete representation of the operating characteristics of a "real" world.

The mazeway may be compared to a map of a gigan-
tic maze, with an elaborate key or legend and many
insets. On this map are represented three types of assem-
blage: (1) goals and pitfalls (values, or desirable and
undesirable end-states); (2) the "self" and other objects
(people and things); and (3) ways (plans, processes, or
techniques) which may be circumvented or used, according to their characteristics, to facilitate the self's
attainment or avoidance of values. For heuristic purposes, let us crudely categorize the content of the mazeway, recognizing that these categories (like the categories represented by different colors, shading, shapes, or

thicknesses of line on a map) do not represent the only possible analytical divisions and relationships. The normal human mazeway, then, may be said to contain representation of at least the following phenomena:

I. Values (images of situations associated with pleasant or unpleasant feeling-tone)
    A. Positive organic values
        1. Eating and drinking
        2. Sleeping, rest, relaxation, absence of discomfort or bodily tension
        3. Sexual satisfaction
        4. Optimal temperature maintenance
        5. Elimination of wastes
        6. Breathing
    B. Positive symbolic values
        1. Testimonials of love, admiration, and respect from human objects
        2. Enactment of behavior-sequences satisfying "in themselves" (e.g., a game or sport, conversation, meditation), or satisfying because they are instrumental to other values
        3. Presence of objects associated with organic and symbolic consummations (including human and nonhuman objects)
    C. Altruistic values (images of situations in which the primary and secondary values of others are satisfied)
    D. Negative values (associated with pain, discomfort, anxiety): the reverse of consummations outlined above

II. Objects (images, with associations, of animate and inanimate objects)
    A. Self
        1. Body image
            a. surface of body

       b. bodily adornment (clothing, cosmetics, perfume, etc.)

       c. organs and organ systems

       d. prostheses (e.g., false teeth, wooden leg)

       e. defects or injuries (e.g., "weak back," "shortness of breath")

    2. Self-image

       a. physiological processes (e.g., digestion, sexual desire)

       b. psychological process (nature of thoughts, dreams, emotions, etc.)

       c. personality (characteristic impulse and action patterns recognized in self)

       d. evaluation (e.g., good-bad, strong-weak) of parts or whole

       e. conception of the soul

B. Human environment

    1. Particular persons

       a. values of others

       b. characteristics of behavior of others (in relation to self and to others)

    2. Classes of persons

       a. particular classes defined (e.g., on basis of residence, kinship, race, political affiliation, wealth, etc.)

       b. values and characteristics of classes (in relation to self and others)

    3. Socio-cultural system as a whole

C. Nonhuman environment

    1. Animals

    2. Plants

    3. Tools and equipment ("material culture")

    4. Natural phenomena (e.g., fire, weather, topography and terrain)

    5. Natural system as a whole

    D. Supernatural environment
        1. Particular supernaturals (e.g., ancestors' spirits, deities, ghosts, demons, etc.)
        2. Classes of supernaturals
        3. Supernatural processes (e.g., mana and taboo, witchcraft, magic)
    E. Statements of how entire socio-cultural, self, natural, and supernatural system works

III. Techniques (images of ways of manipulating objects in order to experience desired end-states or values)
    A. Techniques themselves (an extremely large number of interlocking and alternative statements of "what to do when . . .")
    B. Priority systems among values (statements of which to enjoy first, or which to do to the exclusion of something else)
    C. Priority systems among techniques (statements of which technique to use in order not to obstruct use of another, or the attainment of some other value)

These elements can be combined in an almost infinite variety of "imagined" action sequences.

The concept of mazeway thus embraces, in an organized fashion, several phenomena already generally recognized as common to human awareness: the "body image" (Schilder, 1935); "role," "self," "the other," "the generalized other" (George H. Mead, 1934); "behavioral environment" (Hallowell, 1955); the "world view" (Redfield, 1953). It is reminiscent of Tolman's "cognitive maps" (1948) and of the topological concept of "life-space," and closely resembles certain concepts newly introduced into cognitive theory: the "Image" (Boulding, 1956) and "Plan" (Miller *et al.,* 1960). And the mazeway concept borrows from traditional psychological notions of perception, association, "integration," and patterning of experience. Evidently, in one field the mazeway includes images of phenomena which, to many an outside "absolute" observer, would fall into conceptually distinct and sometimes incommensurable categories: personality, culture, society, natural environment, values, etc. From the standpoint of the individual mazeway-holder, however, all these phenomena normally constitute one integrated dynamic system of perceptual assemblages. Within this system, self and non-self interact according to predictable (if more or less idiosyncratic) "laws," the description of which in generalized form is the business particularly of personality psychology and of dynamic psychiatry.

TABLE 2

ROUTES AND LEVELS OF ABSTRACTION IN CULTURE-AND-
PERSONALITY TERMINOLOGY

1. If one has derived an approximation to a complete description of
       one mazeway, or
       one culture,

2. abstractive operations, involving classification of content into fewer, broader categories, will yield descriptions of, respectively,
       personality, or
       national character.

3. If one has derived an approximation to a complete description of
       one mazeway, or
       one personality,

4. operations, involving addition of all individual cases to the pool of data, without altering the level of abstraction, will yield descriptions of, respectively,
       culture, or
       modal personality structure.

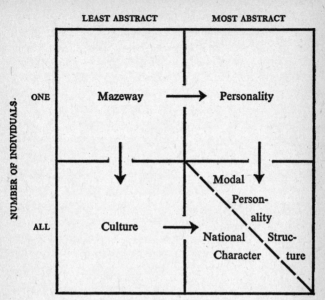

REDUCTIONISM AND THE RELATION OF PERSONALITY AND CULTURAL SYSTEMS

ANTHROPOLOGISTS SOMETIMES like to think of culture as a closed system, and regard most efforts to consider the relation between cultural and non-cultural (e.g., psychological and physiological) data as "reductionism." Leslie White is the most systematic and most eloquent exponent of this tendency, and consequently a discussion of White's position on this matter offers a direct way of coming to grips with the issue. With White's essential position—that culture is "real," that cultural evolution is a major subject matter of anthropology and that the anthropologist should be interested in culture—we can only agree. But some of White's

arguments in justification of this position seem to us to
be not only unnecessary, but fallacious. There are, first
of all, certain questionable ontological claims: on occasion he insists upon settling the question of what
culture *is* by philosophical arguments ("A thing is what
it is . . .") and dogmatic assertions that he *knows* what
culture is and is not. Secondly, the human organism
and indeed all the physical universe are explicitly regarded by him as constant parameters without which
culture could not exist, but which, once given, have no
bearing on the variables involved in cultural process. "A
consideration of the human organism, individually or
collectively, is irrelevant to an explanation of the processes of culture change" (White, 1959). This position
could only be successfully maintained if it were the case
that "the human organism, individually or collectively,"
which White has already admitted is a parameter (albeit,
in his view, a single-valued one) of cultural process,
were indeed a changeless, uniform, absolute, univalued
parameter. But the human organism, individually and
collectively, is not uniform. It has been grossly variable,
in physical evolution, synchronically in any population
in response to genetic, ecological, and cultural circumstances, and in the individual in response to growth,
accident, and disease. Indeed, it is necessary that the
anthropologist take the position that the processes of
culture change (including the process by which human
culture as such emerged) cannot be explained adequately, any more than the processes of cultural function can, without a consideration of the human organism, individually and collectively, and of that organism's
physical environment, as well as of culture, per se. Any
other position will inevitably yield a science of culture
which is no science at all, but a sterile catalogue of
cultural forms.

What sort of consideration of "the human organism" does culture-and-personality undertake in the interest of extending our knowledge of cultural process? First of all, the physiology of the organism is considered, insofar as relevant. The areas of relevance, however, are broad: diet and nutrition; sickness and health; physical evolution; the general adaptation syndrome (of Selye); maturation, sexual differentiation, and aging; psychopharmacology (particularly in relation to narcotics and hallucinogenic agents like peyote)—all of these, and more, are intimately related to both psychological and cultural processes. In regard to psychological subjects, per se, a number of traditional areas are relevant: learning, perception, cognitive process, the structure of affect distribution (a conventional sense of "personality"), and existential phenomenology (the attempt to describe what another person perceives in categories isomorphic with those in which he perceives it). And, most importantly, the human organism is creative: it selects, rejects, seeks information, thinks, makes decisions, and ultimately modifies the systems of which it is a part. In addition to "interacting" externally with other components of social and other systems, the human organism does systematic internal work, the magnitude of which, even in a grossly physical sense, is measured by metabolic assays.

In culture-and-personality analysis, as we implied in the discussion of operational definitions, a society is usually considered to be a system on a higher level of organization than are the individual organisms, or even the social groups, which are the components of that society. Statements about the society—among which are the many statements which constitute a cultural description of it—will be statements about certain properties (including relational properties) of its individual members. Now, if the culturally described system were the only system of which these individuals were components, then a cultural description would be an adequate (for any scientific purpose) description of these several component individuals, and one might well regard society as being logically prior to the individual. But as a matter of fact, individual organisms are also members of systems other than their cultural system. The intersection of a cultural and a non-cultural system, within an individual locus, inevitably generates a third system: the personality system of the individual. This personality system relates cultural to other non-cultural systems.

Why should this be so? It is important to grasp the underlying principle; failure to do so will result in chronic confusion of culture with personality. In more abstract language, we may say that a description of System A will be a specification of certain non-random relations R between certain dimensions of variation a_1, a_2, . . . a_m of component entities, 1, 2, . . . r of the system. These component entities may also occupy other states, randomly in respect to System A, as parts of completely independent systems C, D, and so on *ad infinitum*. The existence of such independent systems, even though they may be functions of the same component entities as System A, do not justify our considering those component entities to be systems themselves. But if a non-random relation obtains between the dimensions of variation a_i and b_j, of any single component entity, which are parts of System A and System B respectively, then not only are Systems A and B parts of a larger system, but that component entity itself is a system (see Figure 1).

In the case of culture and personality, each individual organism must be considered to be the locus of a "real"

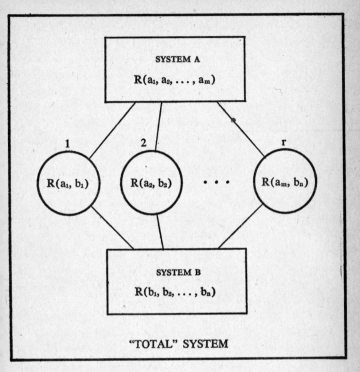

FIG. 1.

RELATIONSHIP OF "HIGHER" (A AND B) AND "LOWER"
(1, 2, ..., r) LEVEL SYSTEMS

personality system, because the states of the organism
relevant to culture are not randomly related to the states
of that organism relevant to a number of other systems.
To take only one example, there is the system of exchange of food and excreta with the physical environment. This requires us to regard the relation between a
culture and any given personality as an intersystem relation and therefore as itself a system. It also requires us

to regard the relation between a culture and any group of personalities as both a set of intersystem relations and as itself another system.

All this is, to say the least, no mean problem for conceptualization. There are available to the student of culture and personality two major, and to a degree antithetical, conceptions of the nature of the relation between cultural systems and personality systems; and at this point, perhaps, the dialectic should be presented, for it will sooner or later be translated into the student's research operations anyway. These conceptions may be construed, respectively, as emphasizing the *replication of uniformity* and the *organization of diversity*. We shall discuss them at greater length later; for the moment, it will suffice to contrast the world view behind each.

THE REPLICATION OF UNIFORMITY

IN MANY INVESTIGATIONS, the anthropologist tacitly, and sometimes even explicitly, is primarily interested in the extent to which members of a social group, by virtue of their common group identification, behave in the same way under the same circumstances. They may for the sake of convenience in discourse even be considered to have learned the "same things" in the "same cultural environment." Under such circumstances, the society may be regarded as culturally homogeneous and the individuals will be expected to share a uniform nuclear character. If a near-perfect correspondence between culture and individual nuclear character is assumed, the structural relation between the two becomes non-problematical, and the interest of processual research lies rather in the mechanisms of socialization by which each generation becomes, culturally and characterologically, a replica of its predecessors. This viewpoint is

particularly congenial to the world view associated with
dynamic psychology, ultimately based on Freud's psychoanalytic theories, but modified by conceiving the
personality to reflect faithfully the culture in which it
was formed and not merely universal constants, such as
the Oedipus conflict and the stages of psycho-sexual
maturation. The sense of tragedy implicit in this world
view is, as everyone knows, very different from that
which preceded it. From the days of the Greeks to the
Industrial Revolution, Western man had, most commonly, conceived of the essence of tragedy as lying in
the inevitability of sin, that is to say, of sacred crime,
the intentional or unintentional violation of "the Law."
Different as are the Greek plays from the Christian
gospels, they agree on one theme: sin is unavoidable.
Beginning with Freud, and increasingly with his suc-
cessors, the inevitable tragedy of man's situation was
not sin, but the conflict of wishes, in themselves neither
evil nor good, and often growing from contradictions
inherent in the person's culture. Thus, to the student
who emphasizes the replication of uniformity, the point
of tragic concern is the fate of those whose cultures,
internally rent with contradictions, instill painful conflict
unavoidably.

THE ORGANIZATION OF DIVERSITY

IN OTHER INVESTIGATIONS, it is sometimes more interesting to consider the actual diversity of habits, of
motives, of personalities, of customs which do, in fact,
co-exist within the boundaries of any culturally organized society. When the fact of diversity is emphasized,
the obvious question must immediately be asked: how
do such various individuals organize themselves culturally into orderly, expanding, changing societies? When

the process of socialization is examined closely, it becomes apparent that, within the limits of practical human control and observation, it is not a perfectly reliable mechanism for replication. And culture, far from being, with the one exception of recent Western civilization, a slowly changing, sluggish, conservative beast, appears to be a turbulent species, constantly oscillating between the ecstasies of revitalization and the agonies of decline. Culture shifts in policy from generation to generation with kaleidoscopic variety, and is characterized internally not by uniformity, but by diversity of both individuals and groups, many of whom are in continuous and overt conflict in one sub-system and in active co-operation in another. Culture, as seen from this viewpoint, becomes not so much a super-organic thing *sui generis,* but policy, tacitly and gradually concocted by groups of people for the furtherance of their interests; also contract, established by practice, between and among individuals to organize their strivings into mutually facilitating equivalence structures. Nor can the phenomenological world of an individual, or of a people, be assumed to be understood by the anthropologist, once he can predict the movements of their bodies; rather, he must recognize the possibility of a radical diversity of mazeways that have their orderly relationship guaranteed not by the sharing of uniformity, but by their capacities for mutual prediction.

From this organization-of-diversity viewpoint grows also a different sense of tragedy. The unwanted inevitability is not sin, nor conflict, but loneliness: the only partly bridgeable chasms of mutual ignorance between whole peoples and the failures of understanding between individuals. A modicum of this loneliness would appear to be as irreducible in interpersonal relations (including the relation of the anthropologist to his subjects) as is the complementarity of perceptions in physical observation.

THE PSYCHIC UNITY OF HUMAN GROUPS

ONE OF THE MOST hoary assumptions of the uniformitarian viewpoint is the belief that a society will fall apart and its members scatter if they are not threaded like beads on a string of common motives. Numerous sources may be quoted which attest to the "common thread" belief. Thus Aberle, Cohen, Davis, Levy, and Sutton (1950), in an essay on the functional prerequisites of a human society, include as prerequisites a "shared, articulated set of goals." Fromm asserts that a nuclear character structure must be shared by "most members of the same culture" in order for the culture to continue; socialization must make people "want to act as they have to act" (Fromm, in Sargant and Smith, 1949). Durkheim's thesis that society depends for integration upon the "common sentiments" of its members is a similar view (Durkheim, n.d.). Honigmann (1954, p. 220) expresses the position in the plaintive assertion, "In any community, there must be some congruence between what different people do, believe, and feel, otherwise social order would be impossible." Margaret Mead (1947a) has carried the argument to the point where cultural heterogeneity (as, for example, in contemporary United States) is conceived as almost *ipso facto* pathogenic:

> . . . in a heterogeneous culture, individual life experiences differ so markedly from one another that almost every individual may find the existing cultural forms of expression inadequate to express his peculiar bent, and so be driven into more and more special forms of psychosomatic expression.

Social philosophers, less humane than the scientists quoted above, but equally disturbed by the problems of their societies, at times have found the "common motive" theme a congenial one, and have used the threat of social disintegration and individual degeneration to justify measures for the standardization of sentiments.

It is, however, impossible to demonstrate empirically that any social system is operated by individuals all driven by the same motives; indeed, the data of personality-and-culture studies, as well as clinical observation, show conclusively that a sharing of motives is not necessary to a sharing of institutions. But how about a sharing of cognitions? Is cognitive sharing a functional prerequisite of society? Here we enter the domain of the ethnographer who may not wish to tread the spongy ground of motive-analysis, but finds it both necessary and painless to make inferences from overt behavior about cognitive matters, such as the criteria for discrimination of kinsmen by terminological category, the substantive beliefs about the order of the cosmos, and the rules of procedure by which a shaman arrives at his differential diagnosis over a sick child. The minimum task of the ethnographer, of course, is simply to describe overt human behavior. "Description," in this minimum sense, is the formulation of a set of statements which will predict, for the ethnographer, what a class of subjects will do and say under various circumstances. Accordingly, any complete ethnographic statement will include a specification of both a configuration of circumstances and of a behavior sequence which a class of subjects produces (presumptively as a result of learning) whenever that configuration presents itself. Usually, the "circumstances" which elicit a certain behavior sequence on the part of one class of subjects will include the acts and utterances of another class of subjects. Therefore, most ethnographic descriptions primarily concern repetitive patterns of reciprocal interaction in which the behaviors of each class of subjects are the circumstance for the behaviors of the other class of subjects.

It has been sometimes assumed that such systems of reciprocal interaction, in which different classes of subjects play specialized roles, as well as general norms describing constant act-and-circumstance relations for a single class of subjects, require not merely a set of cognitive maps, but a uniformity of cognitive maps among the participants for their continued successful operation. Thus, for example, in their previously quoted essay on the functional prerequisites of a human society, Aberle, Cohen, Davis, Levy, and Sutton (1950) postulate the necessity of "shared cognitive orientations," as well as "shared, articulated set of goals." Yet what few formal attempts have been made, by techniques such as componential analysis, to define the cognitive maps necessary to culturally correct behaviors have demonstrated unambiguously that it is often possible for the ethnographer to construct several different maps, each one of which will predict adequately the overt behavior of subjects (*vide* Wallace and Atkins, 1960). Let us therefore now ask the question directly: Is it necessary that all participants in a stable socio-cultural system have the same "map" of the system in order that they may select the correct overt behaviors under the various relevant circumstances?

1. Minimal Socio-Cultural Systems

A system may be defined as a set of variable entities (persons, objects, customs, atoms, or whatever) so related that, first, some variation in any one is followed by a predictable (i.e., non-random) variation in at least one other;

second, that there is at least one sequence of variations
which involves all of the entities.

Let us define the properties of the least complex system
which an ethnographer might describe. Such a system must
satisfy the following minimum requirements: first, that
two parties, A, and B, the initiator and respondent, respectively, interact; second, that each completion of one sequence of interactions be followed, sooner or later, by a
repetition of the same sequence. Using the convention that
the acts of A are represented by the symbols a_i, and those
of B by the symbols b_j, and that temporal relationship is
represented by the symbol $\rightarrow$, to be read "is followed by,"
we assert that the simplest such system has the following
structure:

$$a_1 \longleftrightarrow b_1$$

Since it is legitimate to regard the sense of the symbol $\rightarrow$,
"is followed by," as a reasonable interpretation of the
logical relationship of material implication (whenever x,
then y), we may refer to the structure $a_1 \leftrightarrow b_1$ as a *primary
equivalence structure* (ES_1). In such a structure, whenever
A does a_1, then (sooner or later) B does b_1; and whenever B
does b_1, then (sooner or later) A does a_1.

Interaction structures of ES_1 type seem patently too
simple to serve as useful models of the components of
socio-cultural systems. The *secondary equivalence structure*
(ES_2), however, looks more interesting:

Here, we may interpret acts a_1 and b_1 as instrumental acts
and acts a_2 and b_2 as consummatory acts. The distinguish-
ing feature of ES_2 is that the consummatory act of each
party is released by (but is not necessarily exclusively conditional upon) the instrumental act of the other. The equivalence between a_1 and b_1 describes the repetitive nature of
the interaction. A whimsical but culturally valid example

of a secondary equivalence structure is provided by a little ritual commonly found among the present inhabitants of the eastern coast of the United States (its wider distribution, in time and space, is unknown to me). When a child loses one of his baby teeth, he places the tooth under his pillow at night when he goes to bed; the parent, after the child has fallen asleep, then comes and replaces the tooth with a coin ($a_1 \rightarrow b_1$). The child, on awakening, takes the coin and buys candy with it ($b_1 \rightarrow a_2$). (Possibly, he thereby loosens another tooth, if it is caramel candy!) The parent, meanwhile, after replacing the tooth with a coin, delightedly reports the transaction to his spouse ($a_1 \rightarrow b_1 \rightarrow b_2$). And with the next tooth he sheds, the child, who has observed that tooth-placing is followed by candy and who likes candy, repeats a_1 and thus continues the process ($b_1 \rightarrow a_1$). This simple custom is (for reasons which I shall mention later) not unlike the silent trade, so widely reported among primitive peoples. It may be diagrammed as follows:

More complex structures, involving two parties, can obviously be constructed out of the same relationships. Thus, a tertiary equivalence structure (ES_3) has the form:

Structures of quaternary and still higher degree evidently can be made by a simple process of extension. Structures involving more than two persons also can be designed, although they are more difficult to represent on a plane surface. In general, we can consider that the two-party secondary equivalence structure, which we have suggested as the smallest practical model of a stable socio-cultural system, is only one of a class of equivalence structures ^mES_n, where $m > 1$ denotes the number of parties to the system, and $n \geq 1$ denotes the number of levels of equivalences $a_i \leftrightarrow b_j$ incorporated. It would be interesting to investigate in detail the logical properties of these systems and to speculate that, in principle, *any* socio-system, involving m parties in repetitive interaction, can be described by some equivalence structure of the class ^mES_n. However, these exercises would carry us beyond the purposes of this paper.

We now conclude that the simplest possible social-interaction system that an ethnographer might describe has the form of a two-person secondary equivalence structure. This structure is, however, a model of what the ethnographer perceives; it is the ethnographer's cognitive map. We wish now to discover with what combination of maps, α_i and β_j, held by the two parties A and B, the ethnographer's model is compatible.

2. Minimal Cognitive Maps of Participants in Socio-Cultural Systems

At this point, we must make explicit two conventions which have been employed in the foregoing analysis. These are: first, that the ethnographer's map is valid ("true"); second, that the systems are "perfect," in the sense that there are no exceptions to the regularity of the relationships indicated by the symbols $\rightarrow$. We know, of course, that in "real life" ethnographers make errors and that human behavior is not perfectly predictable. Although it would not invalidate the reasoning to introduce these qualifications (since a probabilistic logic would do just as well as the strict two-valued logic we are using), it would make the demonstrations more tedious. These conventions are now also applied to the cognitive maps maintained by the participants: we assume that each participant's map is valid ("true"); and we assume that the relationships are two-valued ("yes" or "no" rather than a probabilistic "maybe").

We have suggested already that a_1 and b_1 be regarded as "instrumental" acts and a_2 and b_2 as "consummatory." It is important to recognize that this classification is only a relative one; that is to say, a_1 is instrumental with respect to a_2, and b_1 with respect to b_2. In teleological terms, A does a_1 "in order to be able" to do a_2, and B does b_1 "in order to be able" to do b_2. But we do not actually need to invoke any panel of needs, drives, tensions, instincts, or whatever, the satisfaction of which makes an act ultimately consummatory, since we assume that the maps validly describe real events. It is therefore true by definition that neither A nor B will continue to participate in the system unless, first, each perceives that, *within the limits of the system,* his ability to perform his own consummatory act depends upon his partner performing his instrumental act; second, that when he performs his own instrumental act, its function is to elicit his partner's instrumental act; third, that he repeatedly performs his own instrumental act.

The simplest (but not the only) possible cognitive maps for A and B respectively, which satisfy the foregoing requirements, are the following:

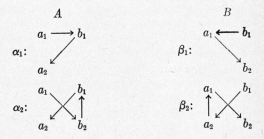

These maps are to be interpreted as follows:

α_1: A knows that whenever he does a_1, B will respond with b_1, and A will then perform a_2.

α_2: A knows that whenever he does a_1, B will respond with b_2 and then b_1, and A will then perform a_2.

β_1: B knows that whenever he does b_1, A will respond with a_1, and B will then perform b_2.

β_2: B knows that whenever he does b_1, A will respond with a_2 and then a_1, and B will then perform b_2.

Each possible combination of these cognitive maps will yield a structure which is identical with, or logically implies, $^2ES_2$. Thus:

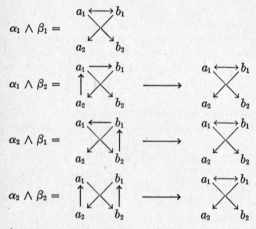

We have now demonstrated that at least four cognitive maps, in addition to the ethnographer's, are compatible with the continued existence of a simple system of social interaction. The four maps of the participant parties can exist in four possible combinations, each of which sums to $^2ES_2$ or to a form which implies $^2ES_2$. Evidently, it is not *necessary* that both participants share the same map; and we have answered our original question: is cognitive sharing a functional prerequisite of society?

3. How Many Combinations of Cognitive Maps Will Yield the Secondary Equivalence Structure?

Even a casual inspection comparison of the ethnographer's model with the four participants' models will suggest that a number of unique cognitive maps are possible which are different from, but contain, either or both of the

A structures, and/or either or both of the *B* structures. The basic model of $^2ES_2$ itself, for instance, contains both α_1 and β_1; $^2ES_2$ added to itself will yield $^2ES_2$; $^2ES_2$ added to α_1 will yield $^2ES_2$; $^2ES_2$ added to β_1 will yield $^2ES_2$, and so on. Let us therefore inquire, out of curiosity, just how many unique combinations of α-maps and β-maps there are where the sum equals, contains, or implies $^2ES_2$, with the proviso that each component α-map include either, or both, α_1 and α_2, and each component β-map include either, or both, β_1 and β_2. The number is well over a million. The number of unique α-maps is over a thousand and the number of unique β-maps is also over a thousand. Thus, it is apparent that even when one considers extremely simple systems, a very large number of different cognitive maps of such systems are, for all practical purposes, interchangeable as system components.

What are the implications of these considerations? Evidently cognitive sharing is not *necessary* for stable social interaction. The two parties to systems of form $^2ES_2$ do not need to know what the "motives" of their partners in the interchange are. Indeed, they need not even correctly know *who* their partners are. In the tooth exchange ritual alluded to earlier, the child at first believes that a good fairy, whom he never sees, takes the tooth, for motives unexplained, and leaves the coin. This relationship is not unlike the silent trade. Later, the child may know that the parents are responsible but does not "let on," from a benevolent wish not to spoil his parents' fantasies about *his* fantasies. One or the other or both of the parties may be able to perform his consummatory act *only* after the partner performs his instrumental act; or other circumstances may also permit it.

But, the advocate of togetherness may argue, whether or not it is necessary that *all* members of society share *all* cognitive maps, they must share at least *one*. Such an argument, however, is not convincing. No criteria known to the writer would specify what one map it is functionally necessary that all members of a given society should share.

Recourse cannot be had to the empirical argument that all members of all societies are *known* to share at least one map, for the data to support such an argument do not exist. And merely demonstrating that some defined group of human individuals, or even all the members of some one society, share a particular map, is irrelevant to the discussion. (Such a society would have to be a peculiarly simple and at the same time clairvoyant one, anyway.) Two or more parties may indeed share a common cognitive map, but such a circumstance is, in a sense, wasteful, since at least two, and therefore all, of these maps must be larger than the minimally necessary ones. And only when each actor is cognizant of the other's "motive" (consummatory act), can the actors' cognitive maps be identical and still contribute to system maintenance.

It may appear to be a bleak prospect to consider that human beings characteristically engage in a kind of silent trade with all their fellow men, rarely or never actually achieving cognitive communality. Indeed, one may suspect that the social sciences have nourished the idea of cognitive sharing for so long, just because the world may seem rather a lonely place if the wistful dream of mutual identification is abandoned. Still another anxiety may now arise: for an implication of our researches is that individuals can produce a socio-cultural system which is beyond their own comprehension. If, for instance, α_k is as complex a map as A can maintain, and β_l is as complex as B can maintain, their sum (*unless* they are identical) will be a structure *containing* $^2ES_2$, but in its totality *more* complex than one or both of them can grasp. If one of these parties be an anthropologist, who is attempting to construct a general ES which he will call "culture," then, alas, he may be a participant-observer in a socio-cultural system which is more complex than he can describe ethnographically! Even if he cannot describe the system fully, he must be able to construct a cognitive map which is more complex than that of any of his subject's.

But perhaps the most significant point to be made is a

relatively practical one, growing out of concerns with the application of anthropological knowledge to psychiatric research. A principal problem for the research anthropologist, in a mental hospital setting, is to explain how a person comes to be extruded from his socio-cultural system. Is it because he is a "deviant," one whose cognitive maps are not shared by other members of the community? Or is it because he has been unable to maintain stable cognitive maps sufficiently complex for them to sum to an equivalence structure with those of his fellows? From the viewpoint of the organization of diversity, it would appear that the most generally adequate explanation is the latter: particularly in a large and complex society, equivalence structures normally will be the articulation of uniquely private cognitive worlds, anyway. The measure of individual survival will not be conformity, but complementarity.

4. Is Cognitive Non-Sharing a Functional Prerequisite of Society?

Finally, we ask whether the fact that cognitive sharing is not a *necessary* condition of society does not mask an even more general point. Not only *can* societies contain subsystems, the cognitive maps of which are not uniform among participants; they *do*, in fact, invariably contain such systems. Ritual, for instance, is often differently conceptualized by viewers and performers; public entertainment similarly is variously perceived by professional and audience: the doctor (or shaman) and patient relationship demands a mutual misunderstanding. Even in class and political relationships, complementary roles (as, for instance, between the holders of "Great" and "Little" Traditions) are notoriously difficult to exchange. Administrative personnel and leaders generally must understand the system on a "higher" level of synthesis than their subordinates, a level which demands a different, because more abstract, cognitive map. Indeed, we now suggest that human societies may characteristically *require* the non-sharing of certain cognitive maps among participants in a variety of institutional arrangements. Many a social sub-system simply will not "work" if all participants share common knowledge of the system. It would seem therefore that cognitive *non*-uniformity may be a functional desideratum of society (although, by the criteria we have used above, it is certainly not a formal prerequisite any more than is uniformity). For cognitive non-uniformity sub-serves two important functions: (1) it permits a more complex system to arise than most, or any, of its participants can comprehend; (2) it liberates the participants in a system from the heavy burden of knowing each other's motivations.

If socio-cultural organization is not necessarily dependent upon a community of motives or cognitions, then by what psychological mechanism is it achieved and maintained? This mechanism is evidently the perception of partial equivalence structures. By this is implied the recognition—as the result of learning—that the behavior of other people under various circumstances is predictable, irrespective of knowledge of their motivation, and thus is capable of being predictably related to one's own actions. Evidently, groups, as well as individuals, can integrate their behaviors into reliable systems by means of equivalence structures, without extensive motivational or cognitive sharing. The equivalence structure model should be congenial to that tradition in social anthropology which interests itself in the relations between organized groups. Thus, reciprocal interactions between the representatives of geographically separate groups as alien as American Indian tribes and colonial or state governments have proceeded for centuries, with only minimal sharing of motives or understanding, on a basis of carefully patterned equivalences. Similar observation might be made of the relations between castes, social classes, professional groups, kin groups, factions, parties, and so forth. In no case is it *necessary* that a basic personality or a basic cognitive framework be shared, but it is necessary that behaviors be mutually predictable and equivalent.

Thus, we may say that as any set of persons establish a system of equivalent behavioral expectancies, an organized relationship comes into existence. Such a system of equivalent mutual expectancies may be termed an *implicit contract,* in the general sense of the word "contract." In this sense, and not in the sense of any formal document, society is, as Rousseau intuited, built upon a set of continually changing social contracts which are possible only because human beings have cognitive equipment adequate to their maintenance and renewal. Culture can be conceived as a set of standardized models of such contractual relationships, in which the equivalent roles are specified and available for implementation to any two parties whose motives make their adoption promising. The relationship is based not on a sharing, but on a complementarity of cognitions and motives. Marital relationship, entry into an age grade, the giving of a feast—in all such contracts, the motives may be diverse, but the cognitive expectations are standardized. Thus, the relationship between the driver of a bus and the riders is a contractual one, involving specific and detailed mutual expectancies. The motives of drivers and riders may be as diverse as one wishes; the contract establishes the system. From this standpoint, then, it is *culture* which is shared (in the special sense of institutional contract) rather than personality, and culture may be conceived as an invention which makes possible the maximal organization of motivational diversity. This it is able to accomplish because of the human (not uniquely human, but pre-eminently so) cognitive capacity for the perception of systems of behavioral equivalence.

Fallacies, Fads, and Specializations

THE PROGRESS OF RESEARCH in culture-and-personality
is, at times, hampered by the common use of fallacious
metaphors and by faddish enthusiasms for particular
jargons and techniques. But it is important to distinguish
between fad and fallacy, on the one hand, and legitimate
specialization, on the other.

Conspicuous examples of the fallacious metaphor are
the frequently mishandled words "internalization," "impact," and "mold." Thus, it is sometimes said that
personality *is* (ontologically) culture "internalized" in
the individual; that culture change has an "impact" on
the individual; that culture "molds" the individual. Such
expressions, and theoretical formulations based on them,
are meaningless in any literal sense. As Radcliffe-Brown
once remarked, "To say of culture patterns that they
act upon an individual . . . is as absurd as to hold a
quadratic equation capable of committing a murder."
As we observed in connection with systems analysis,
culture and personality are constructs of different "logical type," in Russell's sense; that is to say, the concept
of a culture is a set of propositions about some of the
same propositions which are included within the concept
of one or more of the personalities within the society.
Thus, to use transitive metaphors like "internalize,"
"impact," "mold," and so on, to describe the relation
between culture and personality, is precisely comparable
to claiming that a circle has an "impact on," or "molds,"
the points which constitute it, or that the points are
"internalizations" (or "expressions," or "phrasings," or
"transforms") of the equation describing the circle.

The obverse of the "internalization" fallacy is the

"statistical fallacy," which offers an enumeration of the properties of individual persons as if it were a description of a social or cultural system, without any demonstration that a non-random relationship obtains among the dimensions considered. Such statistical "structures" are mere archival material unless a systematic relationship among the dimensions can be demonstrated.

Fads in culture-and-personality, as in other fields of endeavor, are sometimes difficult to distinguish from new specializations. Thus, to some, the projective techniques have been a fad, now happily passing; to others, they appear as legitimate, highly specialized tools which will be continuously refined and employed by a few individuals concerned with particular kinds of problems for a very long time. The fad for projective techniques saw them being used for a time uncritically, as novelties, by dozens of field workers, often in inappropriate situations. Now that the fad stage has worn off and sober reflection has begun, the projective techniques will be used by fewer but better-trained persons for the special tasks to which they are suited, or to which they may be adapted; and we may expect continuous improvement of the tools themselves and of their interpretation as this specialization continues.

A similar observation may be made with respect to a number of conceptual schemes and research procedures "borrowed" from other disciplines. Psychoanalysis, for instance, is a highly specialized branch of psychiatry, particularly successful in dealing with the character disorders and symptomatic neuroses of upper- and middle-class people who can afford and will accept protracted verbal treatment. Much of psychoanalytic theory has been, in one form or another, used by culture-and-personality workers. For a time, it was something of a fad to sprinkle psychoanalytic jargon over the pages of ethnographic reports, like the water of baptism, in order to make them read like personality descriptions. This faddish misuse of psychoanalytic theory, by both psychiatrists and anthropologists, is waning; what remains is a specialized body of concepts and research techniques that will continue to be used wherever profitable by properly trained men. Comparable remarks may be made about the utility of communication theory, reinforcement learning theory, the life history, and other special techniques and bodies of knowledge. Their incorporation into anthropological thought is regularly accompanied by inflated claims that they are universal theoretical or methodological solvents, and students flock to try them out. Enthusiasm wanes when they are recognized as being useful only in solving particular kinds of problems, and they assume the humbler but more enduring role of specializations.

[I I]

The Evolution of Culture
and the
Evolution of Brain

THE CONCEPT OF PERSONALITY generally connotes not only an organization of motives, but also a repertoire of cognitive processes. Contemporary dynamic psychology, in contrast to the early Freudian, is very much concerned with these "ego functions," for they provide the "organization factor" (Rashkis, 1957) which makes the difference between the intricate emotional architecture of mental health and the shambles of mental illness. Furthermore, these cognitive, or ego, functions govern the individual's relation to the world around him via perception, learning, language and other forms of symbolic communication, and by "insightful," "creative," or "imaginative" restructuring. Thus, cognitive processes both organize the motives of the individual and relate them to his environment.

The study of cognition is one of the least thoroughly developed aspects of academic psychology, but it is certainly also one of the oldest (see Scheerer, 1954 for a review of cognitive theory). It is also an ancient pre-occupation of anthropologists. With or without the blessing of psychologists, anthropologists, even outside the conventional culture-and-personality tradition, always have used assumptions about cognitive process as the foundation for culture theory. The rational calculations involved in adaptive behavior, psycholinguistic relativism, the study of "symboling," teleological functionalism, and the rational creativities of innovation—these and similar issues long have been of central concern in anthropological literature. The general point of cultural relativism—that, as Koffka put it, "the fact that things are as they are does not explain why they look as they look"—has been a commonly accepted methodological principle among most anthropologists for generations.

But we cannot here examine the whole subject of culture and cognition. In this chapter, we have a more restricted aim: to consider the implications of the principle that a certain complexity of cognitive apparatus is necessary to the development and maintenance both of the complexity of culture and of the complexity of personality characteristic of modern man. As we look back over the last million years, we observe that recognizably human cultures and personalities have developed in an evolutionary process which seemingly has been dependent upon the evolution of an increasingly large brain. Or, more precisely, these developments have been concomitant with the evolution of an increasingly large cerebral cortex—that part of the brain in which those mental functions which we call cognitive are performed for the most part.

MAN'S EXPANDING BRAIN

LET US FIRST TAKE the long view. In the perspective of the past million years, two major events in the history of the hominids are outstanding: (1) a rapid, progressive, and cumulatively vast increase in the size of brain in certain hominid lines; (2) a similarly rapid, progressive, and vast increase in the complexity of culture in the same hominid lines. These two events, furthermore, have been concurrent rather than successive. It is the concurrence of the changes, in time, that poses the significant scientific problem: the elucidation of the interdependence of the evolution of culture and the evolution of brain.

The probable magnitude of the impact of cultural evolution on brain evolution may be judged from the simple fact that at least one-third of the modern human brain's total volume and one-half of the difference in cranial capacity between modern man and the earliest fossil hominids, the Australopithecines, have been accumulated in the less than half a million years following the invention of chipped stone tools. This is a conservative estimate, based on an assumption of mean modern sapiens cranial capacity at 1350 cc, mean *Australopithecus* at 500 cc, and mean *Pithecanthropus* at 900 cc, and on an assumption that *Pithecanthropus* was the first maker of stone tools.

But this sort of heuristic arithmetic will not carry us very far, and serious conceptual blockages from the start will impede further progress both in defining the problem and in obtaining relevant data. We must therefore examine some of these conceptual difficulties, first from an historical, and later from an analytical standpoint. Such an examination will lead to the chief purpose of this chapter: the outlining of a loose but general theory of brain and culture relationships.

HISTORY OF DEFINITION OF THE PROBLEM

ALTHOUGH THE evolutionary relation between culture and brain may seem to be far removed from the conventional concerns of culture-and-personality, a moment's reflection will show that the subject is not merely relevant, it is central. This is because, as Hallowell (1950, 1956, 1959), La Barre (1955), Henry (1959), Spiro (1954), and other writers in the culture-and-personality tradition have pointed out, the development of man's capacity to form his present kind of complex personality structure is an evolutionary process worthy of study. This process is one which has yielded a brain that is anatomically distinctive in size and structure, most conspicuously in the mass of the cerebral cortex. Increase in size is not, in itself, necessarily a sign of improvement in function, but it is an empirical correlate of such an improvement in the hominid evolutionary series. Hence, in the following discussion, we shall treat gross increases in size—readily observable and measurable—as valid indices of those enlargements of hominid cognitive capacities which have accompanied the evolution of human varieties of culture and personality.

Awareness that the relationship between brain and cultural evolution is problematical has been slow in developing. In the nineteenth century, the matter was handled by citing convenient assumptions. Many nineteenth-century scientists were still influenced by the ethnocentric belief that "civilized" cultures were excreted by "civilized" physical types, and "primitive" cultures by "primitive" physical types. The fundamentalists disposed of the issue by invoking the *deus ex machina*. Darwin, of course, was concerned with applying the same principles of natural selection to human evolution as to the evolution of other organisms. Darwin, however, tended toward uncritical emphasis on sanguinary individual competition for food (natural selection) and mates (sexual selection) as the social processes in which selection occurred; the cooperative institutions were not taken as his model. Furthermore, the supply of spontaneous genetic variations, even in Darwin's eyes, appeared to be inadequate to account for the innovations in behavior which we would call culture today (and which Darwin tended to label as "half-art and half-instinct"). Consequently, he was forced to postulate the inheritance of selected acquired characteristics to account for the differentiation of men from animals and of primitive from civilized men. This led him to an analytical model which has the advantage of recognizing the mutual interaction of brain evolution and cultural evolution, but the disadvantage of invoking the today unacceptable Lamarckian hypothesis. His theory may be exemplified by quotation of the following passages from the last chapter of the *Descent of Man*:

> A great stride in the development of intellect will have followed, as soon as the half-art and half-instinct of language came into use; for the continued use of language will have reacted on the brain and produced an inherited effect; and this again will have reacted on the improvement of language. As Mr. Chauncey Wright has well remarked, the largeness of the brain in man relatively to his body, compared with the lower animals, may be attributed in chief part to the early use of some simple form of language,—that wonderful engine which affixes signs to all sorts of objects and

qualities, and excites trains of thought which would
never arise from the mere impression of the senses, or
if they did arise could not be followed out. The higher
intellectual powers of man, such as those of ratiocina-
tion, abstraction, self-consciousness, &c., probably follow from the continued improvement and exercise of
the other mental faculties.

The development of the moral qualities is a more interesting problem. The foundation lies in the social instincts, including under this term the family ties. . . .
It is not improbable that after long practice virtuous
tendencies may be inherited.

We may smile at the simplicity of some of Darwin's
assumptions, such as the inheritence of acquired virtue,
but the Darwinian hypothesis did not suffer from two
weaknesses which have afflicted some later and more
sophisticated formulations. Specifically, he posited no
discontinuity between evolutionary processes in man,
in animals, and in the transitional forms; and he recognized that what we would call culture today developed
concurrently with brain in some process of mutual de-
pendency.

A. R. Wallace, who independently had discovered
natural selection as an explanatory principle in physical
evolution, sensed another aspect of the brain-and-culture
problem. As Eiseley points out (1958), Wallace had
absorbed, in the course of his travels, some of the
culturally relativistic attitude of ethnology. He used the
concept of culture and he recognized that men of such
"low" cultures as might be found in primitive societies
possessed ample brains. (Darwin naively assumed a
race-and-culture equivalence.) Wallace asserted (quoted
in Eiseley, 1958, p. 311) that

Natural selection could only have endowed the savage
with a brain a little superior to that of an ape, whereas

he actually possesses one but very little inferior to that of the average member of our learned societies. . . . Among the lowest savages with the least copious vocabularies, the capacity of uttering a variety of distinct articulate sounds, and of applying to them an almost infinite amount of modulation and inflection, is not in any way inferior to that of the higher races. An instrument has been developed in advance of the needs of its possessor.

But Wallace himself was unable to do much with his insights; he hinted at mystical, quasi-supernatural interventions in human evolution, and increasingly dispensed with selection (whether of genetic or acquired characters) as a principle to explain the sudden and spectacular evolution of brain, and with it the (supposed) cessation of evolution of other specialized parts, after the upright posture had been achieved. He doubted, indeed, what Darwin and his contemporary (and later) disciples never questioned, that the great increments of hominid intellectual capacity, accumulated since Miocene times, had any survival value at all. But (in common with later evolutionists) he felt that other evolutionary processes had stopped, once the hominid brain had achieved human status (Eiseley, 1958, Ch. XI).

Twentieth-century biology has worked hard to resolve the ambiguities and to prune away the excrescences of evolutionary theory, as left by Darwin, Wallace, Thomas Huxley and other nineteenth-century pioneers. Modern population genetics has indicated that, because of the large number of gene *loci* in man (in the neighborhood of 40,000), and because of the variety of alternatives at many *loci* resulting from genetic mutation, under certain population conditions a sufficient body of diversified genetic raw material exists for natural selection to do its work. It is not necessary to call upon the inheritance of habit as an auxiliary source of variations. Genetic theory has also provided interesting, if difficult to test, theories of evolution which permit, given the necessary data, prediction of the rates and boundaries of change in genetic complexes. Anthropology, comparative biology, and psychology have demonstrated that not only competitive, but cooperative, social systems are common in nature and that cooperative social systems should select for intelligence as strictly as competitive ones. Paleontology and comparative anatomy have documented various phylogenetic histories in considerable detail.

But these developments have, paradoxically, been of little use in the elucidation of the relationship between cultural evolution and brain evolution. The reason lies in the divergence of specializations: biologists, physical anthropologists, and cultural anthropologists have increasingly gone their own way since Darwin's time. Cultural anthropology, in particular, during the first half of the twentieth century, did not maintain intense concern with the theory of cultural evolution; instead, it emphasized close ethnographic description on a relativistic matrix. Both physical and cultural anthropologists eschewed the early "social Darwinism" theories which rather crudely rationalized ethnic, class, and other biases. Furthermore, a philosophic doctrine, central in Darwin's thinking, has been partially abandoned by the biologists. Uniformitarianism, as a guiding principle in the study of man-animal relationships, has been replaced by a concern with man's uniqueness, and that uniqueness has been conceived to reside in man's possession of culture (Etkin, 1954; Huxley, 1941; Simpson, 1949). A traditional, but gratuitous, distinction between "natural" and "artificial" selection further emphasizes man's uniqueness. These currents of thought have conspired to make culture appear to be mainly an epiphenomenon: a product of physical evolution and not a determinant thereof. The problem has been neatly cut in half: biological theory is addressed largely to the explanation of how man came to have a brain big enough to entertain symbols and thus create culture; and what happened to culture and the brain thereafter is, by and large, handed over to the anthropologists (except, of course, by some eugenists who deplore the supposed diminution of the operation of natural selection on cultured man).

Julian Huxley has been perhaps the most eloquent and most popular exponent of the epiphenomenal theory of culture which has, as its corollary, the concept of the uniqueness of man. In a recent essay (Huxley, 1955), urging anthropologists to emulate evolutionary biology in the study of cultural evolution ("the adoption of a broadly similar outlook would permit real progress in anthropology"), Huxley is explicit:

> . . . it appears that before the mid-Pliocene period, some five million years ago, all the purely physiological and material possibilities of life had been exhausted—size, power, speed, sensory and muscular efficiency, chemical coordination, temperature-regulation, and the rest. After nearly two thousand million years, biological evolution on this planet had reached the limit of its advance.

> . . . But evolution was by no means at an end. Major advance was still possible, for other major potentialities of life had not been realized, one of its most important capacities scarcely exploited. . . . [i.e.,] the cumulative transmission of experience. The resultant shareable, transmissible, and progressively transformable tradition gave rise to the new type of entity or organi-

zation technically called cultural, and evolution in the
psycho-social phase has been essentially cultural, not
biological or genetic. (Pp. 6-7.)

Some biologists view the supposed cessation of physical
evolution with alarm. Simpson (1949, p. 334) dolefully
observes:

> Man has so largely modified the impact of the sort of
> natural selection that produced him that desirable
> biological progression on this basis is not to be ex-
> pected. There is no reason to believe that individuals
> with more desirable genetic characteristics now have
> more children than do those whose genetic factors
> are undesirable, and there is some reason to suspect
> the opposite. The present influence of natural selection
> on man is at least as likely to be retrogressive as pro-
> gressive. Maintenance of something near the present
> biological level is probably about the best to be hoped
> for on this basis.

Similar ominous predictions are commonly made by
other biological theorists when the subject of post-
cultural human evolution is broached. Urgent pleas for
eugenic legislation and eugenic education are uttered
in tones implying the imminent end of civilization, if this
negative evolution is not checked by such heroic measures as the sterilization of the mentally ill, criminals,
national enemies, and other "unfit" members of society.

But such oracular pronouncements as these, contained
in philosophical epilogues and popular expositions of
evolution, serve more to obscure the problem than to
clarify it. Actually, they are reassertions of belief in
the continued operation of the selective law, for to assert
that modern culture has eliminated all but "retrogres-
sive" bodily and mental evolution is merely to pass a
personal value judgment on the products of selection.

Of late, however, some scientists have taken up the

problem from the other direction: culture as prime mover and brain as epiphenomenon. Empirical studies have revealed probable continuing evolutionary processes in such genetic traits as blood groups and other racial characters in recent millennia. Dobzhansky, although he repeats the clichés about cultural heredity and the uniqueness of man, emphasizes in a recent textbook (Dobzhansky, 1955, pp.339-340):

> The adaptive advantage of the ability to acquire even the most rudimentary forms of culture must have been so great in the early stages of human evolution that natural selection rapidly propagated the genotypes which permitted the acquisition of culture throughout the human species. The gene-controlled capacity to learn, absorb, and use new techniques and tools was, then, developed, intensified, and diffused by means of biological evolution, making our species more and more human.

Hayes and Hayes, reflecting on the cultural capacities of their adopted baby chimpanzee, went so far as to suggest that man's brain probably increased greatly in size *after* man's chimpanzee-like forebears graduated to a cultural level of existence (Hayes and Hayes, 1955). Physical anthropologists and cultural anthropologists alike have, in fact, begun to consider seriously the role of culture itself as the determinant of man's capacity for culture (see Spuhler, 1959 and Washburn and Howell, 1960 for review of the present status of opinion). A number of anthropologists have contributed to this viewpoint but Tappen first asserted the argument explicitly in a brief paper in the *American Anthropologist* (Tappen, 1953):

> Ancestors of the human group must have made the shift over to symbolic communication to initiate specifically human evolution. Such an adaptive change

corresponds to Simpson's evolutionary mode, the *quantum evolution*. Once such a shift toward this new adaptive zone was initiated, a high selective advantage for individuals better adapted to learned behavior and symbolic communication must have ensued. . . . The progressive increase in brain size is interpreted here as indicating the process involved in the evolution of a species adapting better to a cultural way of life. In terms of selection theory, individuals with better brains would be better adapted to a cultural environment, with resulting superior viability and greater reproduction of culture-adapted characteristics.

Coon, in one of the Cold Spring Harbor Symposium papers (Coon, 1950), has added a significant additional suggestion: that "the recorded changes in the size of the human brain are in some way associated with increases in cultural complexity." A radically epiphenomenal view of culture thus seems, on the face of it, unreasonable, as well as empirically undemonstrable.

THE EVOLUTION OF CULTURE

CULTURE AND PROTO-CULTURE

A. I. HALLOWELL, in a pair of recent papers (1956 and 1959), has observed that a discontinuous concept of culture—as something that came into being with a kind of mid-Pleistocene thunderclap—is fundamentally anti-evolutionist. He points out that pre-sapiens hominids must be assumed to have lived in social groups. The data of primatology indicate that these social groups were characterized by territoriality and by some form of the bi-parental family (i.e., a perennial association of two or more adults of both sexes who, as a group, care for offspring). Enduring, trans-generational territorialism and bi-parental family structure in primates imply not merely learning, but social learning. Furthermore, sub-human primates display various learned skills and have a certain tradition of technical knowledge. They recognize and avoid poisonous berries; they use (but rarely make) traditional implements; they construct and inhabit domiciles ("nests"); they intercommunicate by signs, such as gestures and sounds; they live in bands which frequently are larger than the bi-parental family, and in which a variety of social roles are played by individuals. As Hallowell remarks, such pre-tool, pre-language, pre-fire systems of learned social behavior cannot be maintained by organisms which are incapable of concept-formation (intrinsic symbols); and concept-formation can be demonstrated at least in chimpanzees by discrimination-and-learning experiments (Kelleher, 1958).

Now extrinsic symbols, such as spoken words, are the signs of concepts. Many anthropologists regard the extrinsic symbol as the criterion of culture. Many anthropologists also deny that any animal, except man, is an extrinsic symbol user; thus, they justify the denial of culture to non-humans. But this view is questionable. An animal which forms concepts, and recognizes and produces signs, can hardly avoid associating signs with concepts, albeit on a simple level and perhaps depending more on the language of body movement than the language of sounds (cf., Birdwhistell, 1952, concerning a "lexicon" of kinesic symbols). Etkin, a biologist, in a review of primate social behavior, does concede a limited ability for the use of extrinsic symbols; e.g., a few "words," to the great apes (Etkin, 1954). And some comparative psychologists freely use the word "culture" for sub-hominid behavior systems.

In the presence of these elaborate, learning-dependent social systems among the apes and monkeys, irrespective of the presence or absence of extrinsic symbols, Hallowell, like Bidney (1953), finds it difficult to support the notion of a radical discontinuity. He therefore suggests the term *proto-culture* to denote the systems of socially learned behavior among the higher primates below man, particularly including his proto-hominid ancestors. I would suggest (although Hallowell would not go so far) that the term *proto-culture* be extended, in order to make it logically independent of biological taxonomy, to denote any system of socially learned behavior, irrespective of species, genus, order, or even phylum. While this extension would permit the term *proto-culture* to range over the socially-learned behaviors of various birds, insects, and other creatures far removed from man (a distasteful prospect, perhaps, to those of us who wish to emphasize the uniqueness of our own species), it has the advantage of implying a behavioral continuity between man and other animals. This last implication should also be made explicit: both culture and proto-culture are phenomena of the same class; namely, the class of trans-generational, socially-learned, socially-organized behavior. This more inclusive class may also, in the context of this discussion, be labeled *Culture*.

What, then, are the distinctions between *culture* and *proto-culture*? The fundamental distinctions would seem to be three: the vastly greater use of extrinsic symbols by man, making spoken language possible; the control of sources of energy outside the human body; and the proliferation of technology (traditions of complex manipulative skills in the transfer and application of energy). Language, energy control, and technology would seem to be the necessary conditions for both the self-conscious, self-evaluating, constantly striving, moral character of human society which Hallowell stresses as a *sine qua non* of humanity, and the process of cumulative technical and scientific invention which marks the archaeological as well as historical record. The extensive use of symbols, furthermore, would seem to be conducive to that difference between proto-culture and culture which is of central importance in this inquiry: proto-culture changes relatively slowly; culture changes relatively rapidly.

LEVELS OF ORGANIZATION OF CULTURE

ALTHOUGH COMPARISONS of particular cultures are usually qualitative, concerned with pattern and the presence or absence of specific traits, notions of order and magnitude are continually invoked by anthropologists. Cultures are ranked on single or multiple dimensions, such as level of industrial development, relative competitiveness or cooperativeness, degree of fulfilment of internal potentialities, degree of approximation to or removal from some index culture type (as in acculturation, diffusion, and culture area analyses), absolute level of evolutionary advancement, per capita energy output, absolute quantity of energy exploited, and so on. Simple ranked dichotomies are also often invoked: simple *vs.* complex, primitive *vs.* civilized, low *vs.* high, etc. These rankings are often conceptually metric but empirically non-metric; that is to say, the user of the ranking conceives of the dimension as a continuous variable with measurable intervals between all pairs of values (like the series of real numbers), but the data may permit only a crude rank ordering of values without measurement of intervals. We are interested here in the possibility of treating these metric or non-metric cultural variables as functions of time in evolutionary models.

The mathematical concept of a partial ordering offers itself as a useful non-parametric device for describing evolutionary series. A partial ordering may be defined as a set of attributes so ordered that each successive attribute implies all the preceding attributes. We may for brevity call such a partial ordering a scale. Thus, in the scale $a \leftarrow b \leftarrow c \leftarrow d$, if d is true, then a, b, and c are true as well; if c is true, but d is not true, then a and b are true; d cannot be true without c being true; c and d can be equivalent, and so on. Certain cultural attributes of the primates, as ascertained from comparative psychology and anthropology, closely approximate such a scale, and that scale is in fact both a useful description of the empirical course of cultural evolution in the hominid family line, and a statement of the scaling of cultures among the living primates (see Table 3).

TABLE 3

SCALE OF CULTURAL ATTRIBUTES IN PRIMATES

1. Territoriality
2. Domiciles
3. Band organization   *proto-culture*
4. Bi-parental perennial family
5. Implements
6. Language
7. Tools
8. Controlled use of fire
9. Cultivation and/or domestication   *culture*
10. Urbanism
11. Industrial civilization

The scale of cultural attributes in primates presented in Table 3 is a partial ordering of empirical data, with the qualification that "Language" may properly belong after either "Tools" or "Controlled use of fire." It is, however, non-metric; that is to say, it does not tell us in any quantitative sense *how much* more of anything is contained in 11 than in 10; nor does it even tell us whether there is just as much, or more, or less increment in 11 over 10 as in 10 over 9.

But anthropologists do often place cultures on an implicitly metric dimension (for which, alas, no practical observational devices yet exist): the dimension of level of complexity or level of organization. Coon (1948, p. vii), for instance, explicitly states:

> The essence of the quantitative approach in cultural anthropology lies in the thesis that the main stream or streams of human culture must have proceeded from simpler to more complex. The evidence of archaeology and of history supports this thesis, which in turn accords with all that we know of life in general. It must be equally apparent that the living cultures of the world vary in degrees of complexity, and that whole cultures can be listed and studied with greatest profit on the basis of such a progressive scheme.

Mere complexity, however, is not the best criterion, for in a given system complexity may be accompanied by varying degrees of orderliness. An intuitively acceptable measure of the quantity of organization of a system should increase both with the orderliness of the system and with its complexity. Complexity essentially is a function of the number of possible events within the system. Orderliness, on the other hand, is a function of the relative probabilities of these events. Quantity of organization is the product of the orderliness and the complexity of the system (see Wallace, 1958a for a mathematical definition of these concepts).

In fine, then, we claim that an evolutionary scale of

primate cultures can be constructed on the basis of available data which will approximately fit the model presented in Table 3. This scale probably correlates with a progressive increase in the quantity of organization of the corresponding culturally organized social systems, quantity of organization being understood to be the product of both complexity and order (smoothness of function). Coon, in the work quoted above, describes a series of levels of complexity on a group of (putatively) closely interrelated dimensions, and sums them to define one major dimension of "cultural complexity." This dimension spans points 8, 9, and 10 on the scale in Table 3. The values on Coon's dimensions can be readily translated into the notion of number of possible events: number of occupational specialties in the society; number of institutions to which an individual may belong; variety of articles traded, and so on. Coon apparently assumes equivalent smoothness of functioning at all levels as the parameter of complexity. Other anthropologists, however, have deeply concerned themselves with precisely this notion of smoothness of functioning, using such terms as "cultural integration," "morale," and "vitality." The two conceptual dimensions of complexity and orderliness therefore are themselves conventional in anthropology, and their relationships may be considered without doing violence to anthropological tradition.

RATES OF CULTURE CHANGE

DURING THE PAST 500,000 years or so of human culture history, it is commonly conceded, the rate of culture change generally has been accelerating. Archaeologists contrast the slowness with which the stone tool traditions changed, during the lower Paleolithic, and the rapidity of recent technological changes. Some anthropologists and sociologists, attending to these massive sweeps of time, have suggested that the complexity of various aspects of culture (measured by such indices as number of components in technology), and probably the complexity of whole cultures, have been increasing exponentially. The empirical observation, underlying the assumptions of the exponential model, is that the frequency of innovation in a given field increases with the number of extant components in that field.

When, however, we examine culture change more closely, we find, as might be expected, that this smoothly accelerating curve of cultural-organizational increase is the sum of brief or specialized processes of change, many of which do not fit an exponential model, and which tend to differ markedly from one another in rate and direction. Some glotto-chronologists, for instance, have asserted that the rate of linguistic drift is relatively constant for the "basic vocabulary" of all languages, and that a count of differences between the basic vocabularies of related languages may be used as an index of absolute time elapsed since their social separation. (The logic is similar to the logic in radium-lead and carbon-14 methods of dating geological and paleontological specimens.) Data bearing on differential rates of change are widely gathered and discussed: suggestions are made that some aspects of culture, such as religion and social organization in our own society, change more slowly than others (the "cultural lag" theory); that culture changes most rapidly in the areas of cultural focus; that cultures and civilizations grow, and decline, over centuries, with different rates at different times. Cultural anthropologists, including archaeologists, have been very much interested in the phenomena of diffusion of culture traits over wide areas, the rates at which various culture traits have diffused, and the processes of selection, resistance, and acceptance which facilitate and impede acculturation (the process by which diffusion through an inter-cultural boundary occurs). Recently, considerable attention has been paid to the phenomenon of extremely rapid and widespread acceptance of innovation which occurs in connection with revitalization movements.

These various empirical studies of rates of culture change may, for our purposes, be summarized briefly: changes in the culture of a given localized segment of the human population will tend to be uneven in rate, to the point of being sporadic, and to proceed with different rates (including, occasionally, constant or even negative rates) in different aspects of the culture and in different social sub-groups; furthermore, different segments of the human population at any given time have different cultures, all of which are changing in somewhat different directions and at different rates. These conditions are highly relevant to any discussion of processes of selection in man.

CULTURE CHANGE AND GENETIC CHANGE

IN SUMMARIZING the present position of cultural anthropology on the general relation between genetic and cultural change, in the context of concern with brain-culture relations, four fundamental generalizations may be made: (1) in any given period of time, the human population will be found to exist in numerous distinct societies, many of which are demonstrably undergoing cultural change; (2) during a given generation, culture change usually occurs without concomitant biological change (this view has received classic expression by Kroeber, 1917, in his paper on the "superorganic" and by Leslie White, 1949, in his essays on "culturology"); (3) the direction of future culture change to some extent can be predicted from a knowledge of the present state of a cultural system, and past changes can be plausibly explained in part by describing their antecedent cultural conditions; (4) it is usually the case in culture change that different parts of a population (either sub-groups within a society or different societies within an area of interaction) at any given time will be accepting and using an innovation effectively, while others will not, and that frequently this differential may be related to differential survival and reproduction rates in the two groups.

CULTURE CHANGE AND COGNITIVE CAPACITY

ALTHOUGH SPECIFIC CULTURE CHANGES not only can but usually do occur without measurable concomitant genetic change, it would be a mistake to suppose that culture can therefore be treated as a closed system which, transforming but conserving some mysterious inner source of cultural energy, evolves according to its own plan with neither input nor output. The cultural system is manifestly an open system and phylogenetic change in physical constitution, climatic change, faunal change, changes in physical environment have demonstrably played a part in its evolution, both special and general. The immediate source of culture change is the brain itself, in which changes of state, within the lifetime of the organism, lead to the changes in overt behavior which are the visible substance of culture change. Hence, without evolutionary advance in the brain as an organ, culture cannot exceed a certain degree of complexity because the necessary innovations cannot be made. To summarize the argument in crude metaphor: the Pithecanthropines *did not* exploit atomic

energy, because their *culture* had not yet evolved to the
point where atomic energy was an inevitable next step
in cultural evolution; but *their* culture *could never* reach
this point because 900 cc's of brain is not enough to
produce an atomic physics.

THE EVOLUTION OF BRAIN

IN AN EARLIER PASSAGE we observed that a major increase in brain size has taken place among the hominids
since the invention of stone tools, from about 900 cc to
about 1350 (considering mean values for the most advanced varieties). Let us now plot estimates of mean
values for brain size in the largest-brained species of
primates against geological time. The data are displayed
in Fig. 2. Since the data are of necessity fairly crude
estimates, subject to errors of sampling, errors arising
from unreliable and different methods of measurement
and computation (the use of estimates from living species to represent skeletally similar extinct ones, etc.),
the figures are not precise; the orders of magnitude,
however, would not seem to be in doubt. What is important is that there has occurred in primates "a special
evolution of the brain in the direction of the development of additional cerebral tissue, the weight of which
is independent of body weight" (Jerison, 1955), and
that this "special evolution," as Eiseley repeatedly has
pointed out, has been, not a singular "saltation," but an
evolutionary "explosion." While other orders also show
increase in brain size (e.g., the horses during the Tertiary, as described by Edinger, 1948), the recent primates are unique, both in rate of acceleration and (if
index of cephalization be the measure) in level achieved.

We shall now consider, as the phenomenon to be ex-

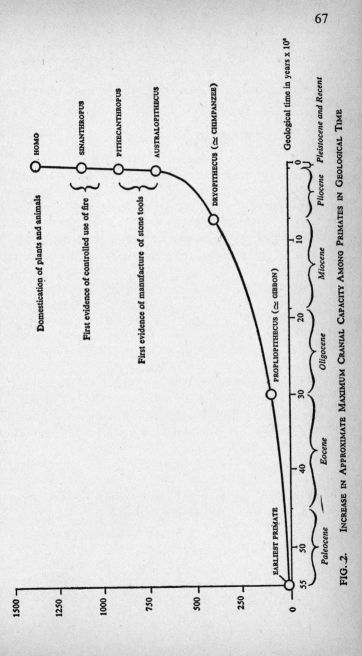

FIG. 2.   INCREASE IN APPROXIMATE MAXIMUM CRANIAL CAPACITY AMONG PRIMATES IN GEOLOGICAL TIME

plained and understood, this unique "explosive," exponential increase in the size of brain, and shall introduce culture change as a possible determinant of this "explosion."

THE DETERMINANTS OF INCREASE IN BRAIN SIZE

THE INCREASE in brain size observable in the paleontological record, and inferable from comparative primatology, is a change in phenotype. Three groups of factors may be, and probably are, involved as determinants: (1) the dependence of brain weight on body weight in phylogenetic process; (2) the dependence of brain weight on environmental conditions affecting ontogeny; (3) the evolution of genes affecting brain size independently of body size.

1. Dependence of Brain Weight on Body Weight

WITHIN MOST of the mammalian orders, brain weight is a definite and characteristic mathematical function of body weight and can be satisfactorily predicted (in an actuarial sense) from knowledge of body weight. But the phylogenetic increase in brain weight, within the primate order, is larger than can be accounted for by the phylogenetic increase in body weight alone. The largeness of modern man's brain, in other words, is not simply the consequence of his having a larger body than his ancestors, although some part of the phylogenetic increase in brain size may be attributed to an increase in body size (Jerison, 1955).

2. Dependence of Brain Weight on Environmental Conditions

ALTHOUGH THERE IS little to suggest that environmental conditions (other than such as produce gross pathologies) directly and independently affect brain size, it is not inconceivable that historical changes in the milieu of the primate brain could be also responsible for part of the phylogenetic increase in the size of phenotypes. Several well-known anthropological studies have demonstrated that changes in the cultural and geographical milieu of populations can affect phenotypic characters, such as head form, body height, and body weight, presumably via such factors as nutrition, stress, and disease. Nevertheless, such factors, undemonstrable as they are, on the face of it would seem to be insufficient to account for more than a small part of the vast increase in size of the primate brain during the past fifty-five million years. Actually these factors could as easily be considered responsible for reducing, rather than maximizing, the phenotypic differences expected from genetic evolution.

3. Genetic Evolution Involving Genes Affecting Brain Size Independently of Body Size

IN VIEW OF the fact that phenotypic evolution in brain size has occurred, and that other processes are inadequate to account for it, it must be presumed that genetic evolution is largely responsible. The genetical theory of evolution, as developed by Sewall Wright, J. B. S. Haldane, R. A. Fisher, and others (see Gerard, Kluckhohn, and Rapoport, 1956, for a summary of this theory), is primarily a rational mathematical theory, rather than an empirical one: that is to say, the equations which describe the distribution of genes are derived from reasonable assumptions, rather than from empirical data, and the entities represented in the equations are not readily observable. Several independent variables, according to this theory, are involved in genetic evolution, particularly mutation, random drift, and selection. It would seem that random drift is unlikely to be the sole explanation: random drift alone, without selection, would tend either to extinction, in small populations, or would be too slow, in larger ones; and mutation rates alone are probably too low to produce the effects observed in the last half-million years. Mutation and selection must therefore be invoked.

This raises the question of the selective advantage of genes conducive to large-brained phenotypes. While it is conceivable that brain could increase in size, not because size of brain is of advantage in phenotypic selection, but because it is genetically linked to some other, non-cerebral, advantageous phenotypic character, it is simpler to make the obvious, if equally difficult to prove, assumption: that brain size, to some significant extent, is correlated with brain function, and that larger brains tend to have an advantage in phenotypic selection. It is not necessary to postulate a close correlation; it is only necessary that the correlation be sufficient to yield the gene for large brain a reproductive advantage under phenotypic selection substantially greater than twice its counter-mutation rate.

At this point it must be recognized that, since it is phenotypes which are "selected" for survival and reproduction, it is probably genetic complexes, rather than single genes, among which selection pressures discriminate most effectively. Thus, in all likelihood, a major increase in phenotypic cognitive capacity must have been the result of the selection of a complex of genes responsible for not merely brain size, but also for size of female pelvis, rate of growth, length of parental life, continuous sexual excitability of the female, appropriate enzyme systems controlling brain metabolism, and so forth; in other words, for that whole set of behavior potentialities that is required for the maintenance of the conditions under which a primate with a large brain can be born, survive infancy and childhood, and reproduce its kind. Undoubtedly, a large number of genes are involved in this process, *all* of which are necessary to the success of the large-brained primate phenotype.

The large number of genes presumably involved carries a further interesting implication: It is highly improbable that any single gamete should be the site of all the necessary multiple mutations; furthermore, since most mutations are recessive, it is still less likely that such a mutational constellation would at once be expressed in phenotypic form. A more likely process would be that of the genetic preadaptation of a whole population, in which the recessive mutant alleles, each with a negligible individual selective value, occurred at random in a population and were diffused by the process of genetic drift. Once the gene pool contained a measurable "solution" of the constituent genes, even random mating, in the course of time, repeatedly would bring together all the ingredients of the criterion complex in single homozygous individuals. Such individuals, phenotypically, would possess selective advantage and would tend to increase the proportion of the criterion genes in the pool, even if several generations of their immediate descendants might lose the phenotypic evidences of the genes. Eventually, however, the proportion of criterion genes would become so large, and the "evolution of dominance" would have proceeded so far, that the corresponding phenotype would be displayed frequently and would be selectively favored in certain local groups, thereby possessing a *group* advantage and eventually outbreeding and replacing other groups.

CULTURE AS A DETERMINANT OF THE VARIABLES
IN GENETIC EVOLUTION OF BRAIN

To DESCRIBE A CULTURE is to describe certain properties
of a population which are closely related to three of the
evolution variables and may be related (at least today)
to a fourth: gene migration, population size, selection
pressure, and (possibly) mutation rate. Let us, for the
moment, discount the last as more applicable to the future than to the historic past which we are considering.

1. Culture and Gene Migration

CULTURE IMMEDIATELY AFFECTS gene migration not
only via a host of regulations on residence and marriage,
but also by the most multifarious and indirect means.
Anything which determines the social boundaries of
sexual relations will affect gene migration: the technology of transportation, the system of trade, the nature of
warfare, religious and magical beliefs, ethnic prejudices,
institutions such as slavery and the adoption of captives,
ideals of sexual beauty, and so on, *ad infinitum*. The
cumulative significance of all these factors lies in their
contribution to the degree of relative genetic isolation
of a culture-bearing population. It is evident that purely
geographical factors affect gene migration, too, by determining the mutual accessibility of populations; but
choice of geographical location, and its significance in
relation to accessibility, are also heavily influenced by
culture. It would seem to be the tentative conclusion of
modern studies that the typical human mating pattern is
for a given area's population to be broken up into a
large number of "partial isolates," within which fairly
free interbreeding is guaranteed (and rationalized) by
prohibitions against marriage between the near degrees

of kinship, as locally defined. This human tendency to partial isolation of small breeding populations, to the extent that it is general and ancient in time, lays down one of Wright's hypothesized conditions for the most rapid kind of evolution.

2. Culture and Population Size

THE SAME SORT of cultural factors which determine group isolation are also active in determining the size of a culture-bearing population. Customs in regard to age of marriage, abortion, contraception, infanticide, and taboos on sexual activity immediately affect the dynamics of reproduction. Age- and sex-specific mortality and morbidity rates are functions of warfare patterns, sanitation, medical care, treatment of the aged, etc. Fertility is affected by nutritional level, occupation, psychological stress, etc., and technology and social structure determine the size of group which can maintain continuous existence as a freely intra-breeding partial isolate. Empirically, the partial isolates, discussed above, for modern European populations range between 400 and 3000 in numbers; among simpler peoples, they are reported to range from 100 to 1500. American Indian "political" tribes (the equivalent of partial isolates), in the northeastern agricultural area, ranged in size from 200 to 6000, with few tribes larger than 3000. Goodenough has shown, with cross-cultural materials, that the size of face-to-face groups ranges between about 13 and about 1000 (quoted in Murdock, 1949). City planners have suggested that, even in a metropolis, the maximum size of the "neighborhood" cannot be more than a figure variously estimated at 2000 to 6000 persons. Since the "effective breeding populations" to which the evolution models refer are bounded not by genetic characters, but by the social relations of the phenotypic carriers of the genes, it would seem that the figures cited above all suggest that the size of human breeding populations, while variable culturally, largely varies between the limits (roughly) of about 100 and 3000 persons. Effective breeding population generally is taken as one-third of the total population. Thus, effective breeding population in humans lies between 33 and 1000, probably tending toward the lower figure in early times at the proto-cultural border, and toward the higher figure only after the neolithic revolution.

If we take these figures as a basis for calculation, we arrive at the conclusion that the total gene pool of any hominid species, numbering 100,000 individuals or more, will be distributed among 100 partial breeding isolates, at the very least. The precise size of the isolates, and the index of their isolation, is largely dependent on culture. In all probability, in early times the number of isolates per 100,000 individuals would have been closer to 3000, since the isolates themselves probably would have been smaller. These conclusions suggest that the typical hominid breeding structure is precisely that envisaged in Wright's hypothesis for rapid evolution: a relatively large population "cellulated" into a number of freely intra-breeding partial breeding isolates.

3. *Culture as a Selection Agent*

WE NOW CONSIDER the effects of culture on the differential reproduction of groups defined with respect to phenotypic mental functions, such as intelligence, educability, concept formation, self-awareness and self-evaluation, reliability of performance under stress, attention span, sensitivity in discrimination, creativity, and so forth. We suspect, but cannot prove, except via comparative psychology, that such functions to some degree are dependent on brain size. In order to simplify our own prose, we shall use the expression "cognitive capacity" to denote any subset of the set of functions mentioned above, on the grounds that they all contribute to maximizing the quantity of organization in the cognitive tasks which are imposed by culture, and that more than simply "intelligence," in the "I.Q." sense, is involved.

The study of culture-and-cognition, as this area of interest may be called, has been slow to emerge, but research is now actively going ahead among anthropologists, linguists, sociologists, and psychologists, in the analysis of the cognitive tasks implicit in minimally adequate cultural behavior. The development of the technique known as componential analysis for the study of meaning, in linguistics and anthropology, and the application to it of the principles of logical semantics, is already yielding fruitful results (Goodenough, 1956; Lounsbury, 1956; Wallace and Atkins, 1960). The description of cognitive task and motivation in innovation, and other aspects of culture change, presents an even more formidable challenge. Initially, it would seem that tension-reduction theories of learning, extended to innovation via the formula, "Necessity is the mother of invention," are inadequate alone to explain all of the phenomena, and that the cultural anthropologist, like some, at least, of the comparative psychologists, will be required first to postulate, and eventually to demonstrate, a primary "play" or "exploratory" or (as I like to call it) "organization drive" (Wallace, 1961). As Linton put it some time ago (Linton, 1936, p. 90):

. . . the development of culture has become an end in itself. Man may be a rational being, but he certainly is not a utilitarian one. The constant revision and expansion of his social heredity is a result of some inner drive, not of outer necessity. It seems that man enjoys playing with both his mind and his muscles.

The skilled craftsman is not content with endless repetitions. He takes delight in setting and solving for himself new problems of creation. The thinker derives pleasure from speculating about all sorts of things which are of no practical importance, while the individuals who lack the ability to create with either hand or mind are alert to learn new things. It seems probable that the human capacity for being bored, rather than man's social or cultural needs, lies at the root of man's cultural advance.

The bearing of these considerations on the relationship between cultural evolution and brain evolution should now begin to be apparent. At a given time, individuals and groups differ, depending on various parameters (such as genetic endowment, health, age, stress level, motivation, and doubtless other factors), with respect to the complexity of the cognitive tasks which they can learn and perform in an orderly way. If this capacity chronically falls below that required by the task, their cultural participation will be restricted, *ipso facto,* and they will tend to be subject to negative phenotypic selection; i.e., they will not survive, or, if they survive, will reproduce at a lower rate. This capacity, it should be noted, is doubtless related to, but is not identical with, "intelligence" as it is measured by psychological tests, since it must include such qualities as reliability of performance under stresses of various kinds; stability of the physiological determinants; preconscious attention span, measured in periods of time up to and including years; readiness to increase performance on call, and probably other qualities which these tests do not generally measure. These qualities will determine, among other things, the *kind* of personality organization of which the individual is capable. Furthermore, it is evident that individuals frequently are faced, in the course of their lifetime, with the necessity of learning new, additional and sometimes more complex cognitive tasks. These new tasks are often presented by new cultural material which has been invented and is diffusing, or is being imposed in the course of change by an interest group or by another society, or is possessed by a competing interest group or society. Such situations likewise bring phenotypic selection for cognitive capacity to bear on a population.

In order to obtain some notion of how selection for cognitive capacity must operate, let us consider the cognitive tasks implied by the controlled use of fire, apparently first achieved by the Sinanthropines with a mean cranial capacity of about 1100 cc. (see Oakley, 1955, for a review of paleolithic fire use). The control of fire by a species has four components: (1) keeping the fire alive over extended periods of time (days, weeks, months, even years); (2) maintaining its size and position within definite boundaries; (3) being able either to transport or to kindle it; (4) using it for some useful purpose or purposes (light, warmth, frightening carnivores, driving or blinding game, tempering wooden implements, keeping away insects, cutting wood and hair, drying wet clothes, cooking, etc.). These four desiderata are both complex and interrelated and they require the cooperation of the group.

Maintenance of a fire means, first of all, bringing to it fuel: wood, or some other combustible material, recognizable from its appearance and tangible qualities. The fire must be close enough to the fuel supply to make the trip convenient. Since not all woods burn equally well and cleanly, the right kind of wood must be used. Furthermore, it must be reasonably dry; and, since in most places where wood can be found, protracted rain occurs from time to time, this means that it must be stored in a dry place. Storage is also desirable to reduce the frequency of trips.

Keeping the fire the right size and in the right place means that it must be large enough to be useful and secure from imminent failure, but not so large as to burn people, food, implements, or clothing, or to smoke out the user, or to use up the fuel too rapidly. It must be insulated from contact with combustible things, such as its own fuel supply, both in order to prevent loss and to keep it from spreading out of control. It must be located where it will not interfere with various activities and yet be where it will be usable; where it will not be in too much draft, nor where it will smother; where it will not be drowned by rain or flood.

Fire must be transportable; otherwise, unless kindling arts are known (and these are of fairly recent origin, coming into use, apparently, long after early *Sinanthropus*), fire-users will be geographically immobilized. Transporting fire requires at least care not to burn oneself, either directly with the brand or coals, or indirectly by firing the prairie or forest. If long distances are to be traversed, special insulating containers are needed.

And finally, fire must be useful. In Sinanthropine times, apparently, it was not used for cooking, but for warmth and dryness, and probably for light and protection. Effective use of open fire for warmth requires that people, gear, and a fire of proper size be carefully placed into a pattern which exacts maximum body warmth from minimum fuel.

In order to accomplish all these tasks, without interfering with other necessary activities, fairly complex cognitive operations are necessary. Types of fuel and location must be discriminated; there must be planning and foresight for replenishment and for such emergencies as rain and high wind; continuous, even if subliminal, attention must be paid to the condition of the fire; infants must be kept from falling into it; and so on and so on. All this, in a group, requires some differentiation of responsibility and also shared responsibility; it requires some instruction of the young; above all, it demands continuous "back-of-the-mind" attention by every member of the group. Language would probably not be necessary, but would be very helpful, for communication and the transmittal of traditional concepts.

Now, from the standpoint of selection, two points may be made: first, a group with fire is, in any environment, in a better position to survive various threats from cold, exposure, and predatory animals than is a group without fire, and will also be able to live in colder regions than its fireless confreres; second, within the group, any individual who is unable to perform the cognitive tasks necessary to fire control is endangering both himself and his group, and he is apt to be negatively selected by his group if he fails to perform adequately. He will find it more difficult to attract a mate and to maintain a sexual relationship; his shivering or baking mate and offspring will have a lesser chance of survival; he himself may be burned or frozen or punished by contempt, assault, or ostracism for his failings. Other things being equal, an individual unable to perform the cognitive tasks required by the social use of fire, in a group in which the controlled use of fire is becoming or has become a culture trait, is less likely to survive and reproduce; but his group (with or without him) has a greater chance of survival than another competitive group without fire.

It is possible to obtain some clues as to the intensity of phenotypic selection for mental faculty in man in modern culturally organized societies. We do not intend to invoke here the commonly asserted, and patently ethnocentric and class-conscious, assumption that number of years of formal schooling, annual income, occupational status, and other such indices of social class are reliable measures of inheritable cognitive capacity. Such characteristics are indeed phenotypic; but their relevance to either heredity or cognitive capacity is very doubtful, and they are more properly described as subcultural differences than as phenotypic evidences of genetic endowment. (Indeed, this sort of class-and-caste eugenics is the intellectual successor to phrenology. Bumps for friendliness, religiosity, pugnaciousness, and so forth, have merely been replaced by genes for farming, banking, college education, mechanical drafting, income over $10,000 per year, and so on *ad nauseam.*) More appropriate for our purposes are gross contrasts between normal and pathological or clinically deficient mental functions (at least some of which do have demonstrable genetic determinants).

We can obtain an initial orientation to this problem by observing that all social groups are forced to make one of four dispositions of those of their members who cannot safely and adequately perform the cognitive tasks required for participation. This disposition may be physical detention (institutionalization, chaining to a post, etc.), banishment, death, or the assignment of a limited (sometimes very useful) role which absolves the holder from some of the general tasks, such as food production, marriage and the rearing of children, military service, etc. But, in general, those of minimal cognitive capacity have both a lower survival rate and a lower net reproduction rate precisely because they cannot perform the tasks necessary to stay alive and reproduce in a culturally organized society. Mentally defective individuals have a much lower life and reproductive expectancy than normals. For instance, in Massachusetts, as reported in 1932, the probability of an idiot female reaching reproductive age was about .2 (by contrast, for a normal female it was about .8); the probability of an idiot female living through the reproductive period was about .1 (for a normal female, about .7). It hardly seems far-fetched to suggest, in the light of these considerations, that even under the supposedly lax and dysgenic conditions of modern urban civilization, cultural selection still operates on phenotypic cognitive capacity with a severity that would be sufficient to produce substantial vertical evolution, in a comparatively short time. This holds true even in cases involving recessive genes, provided sufficient genetic variations are available.

Genetic evolution in brain size may be reaching a plateau, however. The intensity of selection in comparison with mutation rates, and the cellulated nature of the breeding structure, seem to have reduced the hominid store of variability in many genetic characteristics. Straus has cited the remarkable anatomical homogeneity of modern man, including all races, in comparison with wild primates (and, one may suspect, with the notoriously variable extinct hominoids); and Wechsler (the author of the well-known intelligence test) similarly has remarked on the extremely small variance of several human physical and psychological dimensions (Schultz, 1950, and Wechsler, 1930). Indeed, of all the indices of human capacity chosen by Wechsler, brain weight and cranial capacity are the most narrowly distributed—more narrowly, for instance, than intelligence, body weight, or memory span. Little evidence is available to suggest any substantial inter-racial differences in cognitive capacity. If it is true that human evolution has been using up the "capital" of genetic variability more

rapidly than it has been replaced by mutational "invest-
ment," then it would seem that two more conclusions are
indicated: (1) in regard to brain, modern man represents a highly selected and segregated combination of
genetic characters present in small numbers as new
mutants (and only rarely phenotypically realized) in
very primitive and highly heterogeneous, but genetically
pre-adapted, populations (perhaps on the level of *Sinanthropus,* for instance); (2) after this store of variability
in some significant characters has been substantially ex-
hausted, physical evolution, with respect to them, will
perforce slow down in pace to a rate controlled by mutation (if it has not already slowed down, as evidenced
by the relative constancy of brain size since Neanderthal
times). This will, in turn, if not slow down, at least help
to determine the direction of cultural evolution, probably toward the development of cultural systems so devised that machines can take up an increasing share of
cognitive burdens as the total culture increasingly out-
strips individual human cognitive capacities. This process, indeed, is already becoming important. Furthermore, continuing vertical selection for any characteristics
(such as reactions to stress, fatigue, emotion, disease,
etc.) which temporarily reduce cognitive capacity, can
be expected as demands for reliable performance become more intense. This demand for reliability of performance, as opposed to level of peak performance, may
be reflected in the phenomenon of schizophrenia.

CONCLUSION: A THEORY OF CULTURAL SELECTION

IN THE PRECEDING PAGES the relationship of the evolution of culture to the evolution of brain has been examined from various positions. On the basis of modern

knowledge, it seems that several propositions are now reasonably well established:

(1) The distribution of the genetic determinants of cognitive capacity in a population, of which one rough index is brain size, sets upper bounds for the quantity and direction of culture change which is possible without genetic change.

(2) Culture can and does change independently of prior genetic change, within the aforesaid genetically determined limits and, since the protocultural period among hominids, culture has increased in quantity of organization at an accelerating rate.

(3) Culture acts as a powerful agent of phenotypic (and probably of genotypic) selection for cognitive capacity.

(4) Because of the intensity of cultural selection, despite the contribution of mutation, a large proportion of genetic evolution in the sapiens ancestry may have been the result of genetic fixation, at the expense of intra-species variability.

(5) Continuous culture change has probably maintained an especially high selection pressure, and may be producing a plateau, with respect to determinants of cognitive capacity.

(6) Culture change (not, as some theories have had it, just "culture") is probably largely responsible for the observed increase in brain size in the hominid line.

[I I I]

The Cultural Distribution
of
Personality Characteristics

IN THIS CHAPTER, we deal with the aspect of culture-
and-personality studies that has produced the bulk of
the literature in the field. For many people, indeed, this
aspect *is* culture-and-personality. But because of certain conceptual ambiguities, which have given rise to
fruitless controversy and tautology, culture-and-personality studies have reached, in this area, something of an
impasse. We shall attempt to clear away a part of the
debris.

REPLICATION THEORY AND ORGANIZATION THEORY

IN THE INTRODUCTORY CHAPTER, we distinguished two
approaches to culture-and-personality, one emphasizing
the replication of uniformities, and the other the organization of diversity. Both approaches essay to explain
the systems of interaction among individuals by saying

something about what goes on inside them. For descriptive purposes serving only to delineate the preponderant characteristics of a group, particularly in comparing them with some other group (e.g., in comparing one tribe with another, or one generation with another), the replication-of-uniformity approach is convenient and serviceable. But for the purpose of developing empirical support of theoretical analysis of the relation of sociocultural and personality systems, the organization-of-diversity approach is essential. And contrawise, in such contexts the replication-of-uniformity approach is misleading.

One extreme formulation of the replication approach is so nearly tautological as to make empirical investigation unnecessary. This is the microcosmic metaphor. It takes many forms, but they convey in common the proposition that inside the head of "the —————" (adjectival form of name of group inserted here) is a little replica of his group's culture, systematically transformed, point for point, to fit neural tissue, which he has "internalized." This replica is "the —————" personality. With some such formula in mind, it has been asserted that "all culture and personality studies . . . are focused on the way human beings embody the culture they have been reared in, or to which they have immigrated" (Mead, 1953). To a few persons, in every group, of course, the formula does not apply; these few may be called "deviants." Such deviants excluded, the metaphor implies, first of all, a conformity of all personalities within a given culture-bearing (or subculture-bearing) group to a single personality type; second, it implies a perfect association between culture type and personality type. From the latter assumption, accordingly, inference can supposedly proceed in two ways: culture can be deduced from personality, and personality can be deduced from culture. The process by which the internalization is accomplished is the process of child development as it is phrased in the given culture.

The confusions produced by attempting to interpret empirical data from the standpoint of the microcosmic metaphor are well exemplified in a famous analysis of Alorese personality materials (Du Bois, 1944). The psychoanalytic consultant, working with field data brought back by the anthropologist, assumes that all Alorese share a basic personality structure because all have been exposed to the same cultural influences. But he also finds empirically that each of the four males, from whom autobiographical and dream material were secured, is a "highly individual character." "Each has some features of the basic personality structure, but each in turn is molded by the specific factors in his individual fate." The analyst, in fact, has great trouble in relating the character structures of his four males to any basic personality norm. Thus, on initial presentation, he observes, "It is difficult to decide how typical Mangma is. I would venture to say that if he were typical, the society could not continue to exist." Yet, later he asserts, "Mangma is the most typical, and his character corresponds to the basic personality structure." Rilpada, a second male, is "atypical" because he is passive and has a strong super-ego, owing to a good maternal care and a powerful father. (The typical male Alorese super-ego is "of necessity" weak.) Fantan, a third, has "the strongest character formation, devoid of inhibitions toward women." Fantan "differs from the other men . . . as much as a city slicker differs from a farmer." (The basic personality structure "for males," as the analyst defines it, is extremely inhibited in regard to heterosexuality: "the approach to the woman is filled with shyness and anxiety.") Malelaka is likewise difficult to evaluate. The analyst says, "His life history is in every way typical." This is remarkable, because Malelaka was a notorious prophet who attempted to launch a religious revival. On the other hand, he is said to be similar to Rilpada, another seer, who in turn was described as "atypical." And to complicate things still further, the analyst says that "characters such as Mangma, Rilpada, and Fantan can be found in any society."

The microcosmic metaphor is generally invoked in the cultural deductive method, which involves subjecting ethnological description to psychological analysis. In this method, the anthropologist's, historian's, or folklorist's accounts of myth and legend, religious ritual, economic relations, and so forth, are "interpreted" according to some schema, usually psychoanalytic, which treats these behaviors as if they were the neurotic productions of a single individual. This has been the particular interest of those culturological psychoanalysts who deduce from the cultural materials, with the help of psychoanalytic theory, the "meaning" of various institutions to the individual member of the society. Criticism of this procedure has sometimes been savage, since the interpretations themselves at times seem to be arbitrary, if not farfetched, and demonstration that they are validly attributable to all, or even more than a few members of the society, is invariably lacking. *Ad hominem* argument may even displace rational discussion between antagonists in such discussions!

Rational criticisms of the microcosmic metaphor would seem to fall into three categories: (1) that the metaphor implies a false equivalence between concepts on different levels of abstraction (e.g., a personality is no more an embodiment of the culture than a baby is an embodiment of the birth rate); (2) that the metaphor is simplistic (there is far greater variability in personal characteristics than can be accounted for by the formulas); (3) that there is no reason to suppose that social organization requires a high degree of personal conformity to universalistic norms (e.g., the relations between males and females depend not on mutual conformity to one role, but on a complementarity of different roles).

Rational defenses of the microcosmic position have, however, been vigorous. Most of its proponents admit freely that every individual, even in the most uniformitarian society, is somewhat different from every other, as a result of the interplay of various genetic factors and the accidents of experience. But this diversity, as it is described, reminds one of the "diversity" of houses in a new development: the paint is of different colors, and the roof-line rotates from house to house through a ninety-degree arc, but the floor plans are all the same. In other words, the dynamically important features are assumed to be the ones which are shared. Thus, despite lip service to individual variations, the notion of "statistical" distribution is still resisted. Margaret Mead, for instance, has insisted that descriptions of individual characteristics and of cultural setting be so precise that perfect co-variation is obtainable between them. "Any member of a group, provided that his position within that group is properly specified, is a perfect sample of the group-wide pattern on which he is acting as an informant. . . . Any cultural statement must be made in such a way that the addition of another class of informants previously unrepresented will not change the nature of the statement in *a way which has not been allowed for in the original statement*" (Mead, 1953). But assertions that one component is a "perfect sample" of a pattern, once the component's relations to the other components have been specified, means no more than saying that one bead is a perfect sample of a wampum belt, if one already has the wampum belt in one's hand. The question of distribution has simply been begged by sampling other informants to specify the "sample" informant's "position."

But, while the "cultural sampling" defense is logically weak, it is related to another proposition which has merit of its own, independent of its status in this argument (in which it is both a strong and a weak defense). This defense is the notion of "pattern" itself. "Pattern" has at least two senses in culture-and-personality writing: a sense in which it is a synchronic complex common to diverse representations, and a sense in which it is a diachronic complex common to diverse sequences. A pattern is, of course, a class of phenomena susceptible of many sub-classes, which in themselves are of interest; but its identity as a recognizable class cannot be questioned merely because it contains sub-classes. The strength of the pattern concept, as a defense of the microcosmic view, is that the existence of a pattern cannot be properly denied, merely by insistence on differentiating and counting the frequences of its sub-classes. Its weakness is the weakness of the old comparative method: the analyst, only too easily, can take a piece from here, a shred from there, and relate them intuitively, by such methods as "end linkage" and "resonance" analysis (Mead and Metraux, 1953), in a pattern whose locus rests undefined. The old cultural evolutionists, as has often been said, would take a custom from this tribe, and a legend from that, and by patiently fitting together such bits and pieces, would construct a culture pattern (a "stage" of cultural evolution) which may never have existed anywhere, and certainly was not a part of the heritage of all known cultures. The pattern analysts in culture-and-personality are

prone to take a childhood memory from this informant,
a neurotic phobia from that, the theme from a movie,
and the history of an international incident and, by
skillful maneuvering of the pieces, produce a "pattern"
which is discoverable in no one individual but is attributable to all. The deficiency in this procedure springs
not from any lack of comprehensiveness of the observations on which it is based, nor from any lack of reliability in the processes of combining elements to form patterns, but in the *non sequitur* by which such a pattern is
ascribed to uninvestigated (and sometimes, as in the
Alorese case, even to investigated) individuals en masse.

There exists a parallel tradition, stemming from Sapir
(Mandelbaum, 1949) and Hallowell (1955) more than
from Mead and Roheim, which partially avoids the pitfalls of the microcosmic metaphor by giving more emphasis to the uniqueness of the individual. Sapir was
impressed by the fact that individual informants gave
different information and that no one informant knew
the whole culture. "Two Crows denies this," meant, for
Sapir, that Two Crows "had" a different culture, and
probably a correspondingly different personality, from
the other informant (Mandelbaum, 1949). Spiro
(1951) similarly has emphasized the uniqueness of private family and individual cultures, each as the product
of a particular history of social interaction of the individuals being considered. But the logical consequence
of this line of reasoning is another impasse: even though
individual differences are more fully recognized, culture
again becomes merely the subjective microcosm of personality, a distinction between the two is a "false dichotomy," and we are back where we started, with culture
and personality paired off as equivalent constructs.

An alternative is the organizational theory. According to this viewpoint, no population, within a stated cul-

tural boundary, can be *assumed* to be uniform with respect to any variable or pattern. (For example, it cannot be *assumed* that males and females share the same values, the same role cognitions, the same emotional structure.) In every instance, a distribution will be found to characterize the sample. Personality is not assumed to be an internalization of the culture, and culture is not conceptualized as a constant environment, or projection, of all members of the society. Both personality descriptions and cultural descriptions are considered to be intuitive or formal abstractions by an observer from mazeway descriptions of individuals. Individual personality constructs are generalizations about one individual's mazeway over time; cultural constructs are generalizations and syntheses of behavior which is shared by, and/or produced by, groups. Modal personality and national character are abstractions from personality and cultural data respectively. There is no finite list of categories which define personality, nor any specified number or proportion of individuals who must share behavior for it to be called "culture." Descriptions of culture will include statements of relations between behavior patterns which no informant has given or is able to give: cultural descriptions need not be "psychologically real" (Wallace and Atkins, 1960) to the informant.

The consequences for theory and for empirical study of taking the microcosmic or the organizational viewpoint are large, and it is this fact which makes discussion of the problem important. If the microcosmic view is adopted, then research is not necessary to demonstrate that co-variation between personality and culture is exact (given constant "genetic factors"); this is regarded as true by definition. The problem becomes essentially one of child development: *how* does the child come to "embody" his culture? Hence, many of those who take the microcosmic view are pre-eminently interested in child training, education, and so forth. If the organizational view is adopted, however, then (as we have suggested in the Introduction) the problem of greater interest is the processes by which individually diverse organisms work to maintain, increase, or restore quantity of organization within their own psychological systems and within socio-cultural and physical systems of which they are components. Child development remains a significant problem, but is no longer to be considered as the only focal one. Statements about "the ————" and his cultural and personal characteristics may still be made, but they are now understood as conveniently brief expressions for more cumbersome formulations specifying sub-group membership and relative frequency.

Synchronic Distributions

Synchronic distributional studies of personality attempt to answer the question: At a given point in time, what is the frequency distribution of certain personal characteristics in a certain class of persons? "Class of person" is defined by the possession, by *all* the persons in the class, of some property in common: a nationality ("Japanese"), a race ("Mongoloid"), a region ("the southern United States"), an age group ("persons over sixty-five"), a civilization ("Western culture"), a culture area ("the Plains Indians"), a social class ("the bourgeoisie"), an ethnic group ("second generation Italian-Americans"), a religion ("conservative Judaism"), an economic status ("families with an average yearly income of less than 2000 dollars"), an occupation ("waiters"), a sex ("female"), a tribe ("the

Ojibwa"), a community ("Plainville, U.S.A."), or, in fact, any one or combination of an indefinitely large number of possible properties. Many of these class-defining properties are non-cultural (e.g., "age"), but since all are likely to be related to variation in cultural systems, they are met with in culture-and-personality studies.

The panel of personal characteristics used in culture-and-personality studies is as large as the panel of classes. The psychology of personality has yielded many systems, concepts, and measurement devices. These various schemata, as we indicated in the Introduction, do not claim exclusive validity; rather, they are relevant and appropriate to different practical purposes and operational situations. But all have in common, at least, a connotation of concern with that structure of relatively abstract values, and their means of achievement, that is maintained by an individual over a protracted time. We may classify them with respect to the technique of investigation (projective test, depth interview, galvanic skin response, free association, questionnaire, etc.), or analytical schema (authoritarian vs. democratic, introversion vs. extroversion, the psychoanalytic dynamic characterology, and so forth). Within anthropology, perhaps the most commonly employed analytical frames have been the following: genius (as of a culture or civilization), world view, ethos, themes, values, national character, basic personality structure, and modal personality structure. Technically, some of these are largely constructed by abstraction from individual personality descriptions, and others by deduction from cultural descriptions. Some emphasize cognitive positions (beliefs); others, affective orientation (emotional tone) and motivation. Now let us briefly discuss each analytical frame separately.

"GENIUS"

MOST ABSTRACT and least affective in content is a set of psychological characteristics, usually inferred from cultural data, which may, for want of a better term, be labeled "genius," in the sense connoted by such expressions as "the genius of Greek civilization." It is probably in psycho-linguistics, following the tradition set by Sapir and Whorf, that the theory behind this approach is most rigorously developed; but Kroeber, Spengler, Toynbee, and other philosophers of history have been concerned to capture its essential theme. The genius of a people has both a continuous and an evolutionary aspect. Its continuity is provided by the constant presence, throughout an extended historical process, of a definite frame of reference that provides certain primitive categories into which experience can be coded, and defines the kinds of relationships which conceivably can exist between such categories. Thus, it functions (in theory at least) as a set of parameters or rules governing mental operations. In this sense, genius can be compared to the primitive predicates, operators, and axioms of a logical calculus; once established, only certain propositional functions can be constructed; indeed, only a finite number of these functions is possible. In its evolutionary sense, the genius of a people is the plot or program which is displayed in its history: the unfolding, over centuries or millennia, of the inner potentialities of the primitive cultural axioms. Here again, the comparison to a logical calculus is apt, for the plot of a culture unfolds in a way comparable to the gradual unfolding, in logical and mathematical discovery and proof, of new theorems, each of which serves as the basis for further cumulative synthesis. Thus, genius is like a geometry, being expressible both in its primitive axiomatics and in the historical process of theorem development. Ultimately, of course, an end may be reached, when the genius has fulfilled its destiny, and a phase of sterility ending in "death" supervenes.

Thus, the concept of genius often has both a mystical, fatalistic quality, best expressed by philosophers of history such as Spengler, and a hard and logical quality, voiced by psycho-linguists such as Whorf and by culturologists such as Kroeber and White. It is both the "soul" of the super-organic and the phonemics, lexicon, and syntax of culture, depending on the use to which the concept is being put.

Examples of descriptions of genius, in its continuous and evolutionary aspects, will make the concept clear. Whorf (1956, pp. 57-58), for instance, describes certain features of the genius of the Hopi in their continuous aspects. He derives his data from an intensive examination of the Hopi language:

> After long and careful study and analysis, the Hopi language is seen to contain no words, grammatical forms, constructions or expressions that refer directly to what we call "time," or to past, present, or future, or to enduring or lasting, or to motion as kinematic rather than dynamic (i.e., as a continuous translation in space and time rather than as an exhibition of dynamic effort in a certain process), or that even refer to space in such a way as to exclude that element of extension or existence that we call "time," and so by implication leave a residue that could be referred to as "time." Hence, the Hopi language contains no reference to "time," either explicit or implicit.
>
> At the same time, the Hopi language is capable of accounting for and describing correctly, in a pragmatic or operational sense, all observable phenomena of the universe. . . . Just as it is possible to have any number

of geometries other than the Euclidean which give an equally perfect account of space configurations, so it is possible to have descriptions of the universe, all equally valid, that do not contain our familiar contrasts of time and space. The relativity viewpoint of modern physics is one such view, conceived in mathematical terms, and the Hopi Weltanschauung is another and quite different one, nonmathematical and linguistic. . . .

This analysis of Whorf's, and comparable exercises by other psycho-linguists, was explicitly recognized by Whorf as an approach to understanding psychological processes. As Whorf put it:

. . . linguistics is essentially the quest of MEANING. It may seem to the outsider to be inordinately absorbed in recording hair-splitting distinctions of sound, performing phonetic gymnastics, and writing complex grammars which only grammarians read. But the simple fact is that its real concern is to light up the thick darkness of the language, and thereby of much of the thought, the culture, and the outlook upon life of a given community, with the light of this "golden something," as I have heard it called, this transmuting principle of meaning. As I have tried to show, this amounts to far more than learning to speak and understand the language as the practical language teacher conceives these ends. The investigator of culture should hold an ideal of linguistics as that of a heuristic approach to problems of psychology which hitherto he may have shrunk from considering—a glass through which, when correctly focused, will appear the TRUE SHAPES of many of those forces which hitherto have been to him but the inscrutable blank of invisible and bodiless thought (1956, p. 73).

From this point of view, therefore, linguistics becomes a method for investigating what may be termed the semantic geometry of culture. It may be doubted whether structural linguistics per se is fully equipped to conduct such investigations; but such further, semantically directed, procedures as are offered by componential analysis (Goodenough, 1956; Lounsbury, 1956; Wallace and Atkins, 1960), in combination with lexical and grammatical analysis *a la* Whorf, can make rigorous investigation possible.

In the evolutionary sense, genius is the program of development of a logical system: the successive working out of the theorems, as it were, which are implied by the axioms of the semantic geometry. Kroeber, in his study *Configurations of Culture Growth* (1944), in his outline of native North American culture areas (1939), and in various other places, has pointed out that the histories of cultures display a characteristic sequence of rise, climax, and fatigue. He suggests that this sequence is the program of the working out of the "logical possibilities" of particular "styles" or "patterns." The analysis (Kroeber, 1948, pp. 330-331) of the development of Greek mathematics is typical:

> We have seen that Greek science and mathematics came in a four-century spurt and then stood still. The Greeks never did achieve much in simple arithmetic, probably partly because their method of writing quantities—by letter symbols denoting certain specific numbers instead of by position numerals—made ordinary computations of any size difficult. Even less was accomplished by them in algebra, of which the imperfect rudiments began—or first appear to our view—some four hundred years after Greek general mathematical progress had stopped. The branch of mathematics the Greeks did wholly originate and develop was geometry —plane, solid, and spherical. Here they substantially "exhausted the pattern," fulfilled its possibilities, and left nothing for others to discover. Now geometry is a

special way of doing mathematics—with a compass and rule and nothing more, the Greeks insisted. It visualizes properties and relations; it can be pictured, as algebra and arithmetic cannot be. Although already truly abstract, geometry easily retains the most concrete aspect of all branches of mathematics. This geometric approach was the Greek "style" in mathematics. One part of the style was the Greek emphasis on proportion, which can also be diagramed; and the Greek avoidance, where possible, of all but integral numbers, which can be handled like visible and tangible blocks; and the avoidance also of negative quantities and irrational fractions, which cannot be handled in this way. On the positive side, again, the Greeks pushed on from their geometry into conic sections—dealing with plane cuts across cones, resulting in curves such as ellipses, parabolas, hyperbolas. This is a branch of mathematics which we still call by the original name of "conic sections," although we mostly express its concepts algebraically now. The further limitations of the mathematical style of the Greeks are shown by their failure to develop anything at all in the field of logarithms, analytical geometry, calculus, or the concept of function. What they could do with their geometrical and whole-numbered manner of style, they achieved. Other mathematical possibilities, like these mentioned, were simply left to be realized by other peoples and times—chiefly by western Europeans in the last three or four centuries.

Kroeber's type of analysis applies equally well to other categories of culture and, indeed, to the "style" (or genius) of whole civilizations.

In sum, then, we can define the "genius" of a population as a set of highly generalized primitive concepts and axioms which serve as the frame of reference for a whole society (or, at least, a large portion thereof). These axioms may, themselves, not be consciously recognized by their holders and, in general, may be abstracted from cultural or psychological data. They imply the program of possible cultural evolution and thus set limits on possible cultural development by the population which entertains them.

WORLD VIEW

STILL PREDOMINANTLY COGNITIVE, but more concrete in reference to observable things, is world view. The concept of world view has been most effectively developed by Robert Redfield and others associated with him. It primarily refers to cognitive content, some of which may be affectively neutral, and is derived by abstraction from ethnographic description. Redfield defines world view (Redfield, 1952, p. 30) as that outlook upon the universe which is characteristic of a people:

"World view" differs from culture, ethos, mode of thought, and national character. It is the picture the members of a society have of the properties and characters upon their stage of action. While "national character" refers to the way these people look to the outsider looking in on them, "world view" refers to the way the world looks to that people looking out. Of all that is connoted by "culture," "world view" attends especially to the way a man, in a particular society, sees himself in relation to all else. It is the properties of existence as distinguished from and related to the self. It is, in short, a man's idea of the universe. It is that organization of ideas which answers to a man the questions: Where am I? Among what do I move? What are my relations to these things?

But Redfield does not really mean *any* existential belief; he is referring to broad classes of such beliefs. Thus, it is very similar to the concept of "implicit dominant ontology," which refers to the major assumptions about the existential nature of the world that are held by a population, and to "cosmology" which may be conceived as a systematized world view. Redfield regards some categories of world view as psychic universals: belief in a division of things into those that are self and those that are non-self; in a division of the latter into human, non-human but material, and supernatural; in distinctions between earth and sky, day and night, birth and death, etc. Among the multitude of world views which the anthropologist may observe, Redfield pays particular attention to one kind: the primitive world view, said to be characterized by three major assertions: (1) that the distinction between the self and that which the self confronts is blurred, so that man tends to see himself as united with nature, rather than standing apart from it; (2) that man participates in maintaining this unitary system of man-in-nature, rather than dominates or changes it; (3) that the universe is morally significant, because all of nature is animate and hence man's relationship with nature, like all social relationships, must be moral.

Other scholars, of course, have dealt with comparable concepts in contrasting primitive and civilized, folk and urban, provincial and cosmopolitan, and so forth. When Cassirer (1946) describes the "mythopoeic personality" of the primitive; when Hallowell (1955) discusses time and space orientation among the Ojibwa; when Wallis (1930), Lowith (1949), and Bury (1921) consider concepts of eschatology and progress; when Weber (1930) analyzes the Protestant ethic; when Mannheim (1936) discusses ideologies and utopias, each is dealing with world view.

Mention of Mannheim must turn the reader's attention to the traditional interest of Continental sociologists in the sociology of knowledge. The essential theme of Mannheim's work is thoroughly at home in anthropological theory: that the whole fabric of institutions of a society must be intimately related to the dominant system of existential belief which, in turn, not merely rationalizes, but springs naturally from the exigencies of functional organization. Thus, a world view is not merely a philosophical by-product of each culture, like a shadow, but the very skeleton of concrete cognitive assumptions on which the flesh of customary behavior is hung. World view, accordingly, may be expressed, more or less systematically in cosmology, philosophy, ethics, religious ritual, scientific belief, and so on, but it is implicit in almost every act. In Parsonian terms, it constitutes the set of cognitive orientations of the members of a society (Parsons and Shils, 1952).

VALUES, ETHOS, AND THEMES

SOMETHING OF VALUE is something which an organism will work to experience. "Values" as such, however, as abstract entities, are rather difficult to define. In one sort of economic usage, "the value" of anything is, in a sense, an intangible property added to a raw, primitive material by a producer who performs work upon it and by a consumer who performs work to obtain it. The measure of this added value is a function of both the producer's and the consumer's work. In psychological, sociological, and anthropological usage, the "value" of a thing or a state of affairs is, somewhat comparably, its positive or negative valence, i.e., its relative potency as a goal ("reward," "punishment," "pleasure," "pain," etc.) toward which, or away from which, the organism strives. An object which has acquired psychological value is said to have been "cathected." Thus, the "value" of a long life, or food pellets, or sexual satisfaction, or membership in a prestigeful group, or whatever, can be stated as a quantity, or at least as a rank order, on a scale from minus-x through zero to plus-x. But "a value," in the sense of the term used by psychologists, anthropologists, and sociologists, means more than the cathexis figuratively clinging, like a charge of positive or negative static electricity, to some object. First of all, "a value" refers not merely to the cathectic "charge," but also to that which bears the "charge"—the mental image, or the object itself, which is the goal ("consummatory values") and, sometimes, even to behavioral gambits which the organism may employ to approach or avoid it ("instrumental values"). Secondly, because "values" in the latter sense are closely related to ontology, empirical descriptions of "values" tend to include descriptions of genius and world view (cf. Rapoport, 1954). Finally, in anthropological usage, "the values" of a people, or a culture, are not really any and all object-cathexes, but only those which the anthropologist can show to be widely shared, to be considered "desirable," as well as merely "desired," and to pervade many different cultural categories: in a word, they are abstractions or logical types of very high order.

The concept of values sometimes appeals to social anthropologists who, for one reason or another, do not feel comfortable with personality psychology. In particular, as criticism of the uniformitarian implications of some national character studies has mounted, the concept of values has provided a kind of substitute. "Personality" may be variable, but are not the "values" of a people shared? And are not "values" somehow more impersonal, more structural, more clearly relevant to culture? Do not certain "values" organize the diversity of personalities in society?

The most extensive use of the concept of *values* by anthropologists has been made in Harvard University's Comparative Study of Values in Five Cultures (Navaho, Zuni, Mormon, Texan, and Spanish-American). The Study works with broad values, such as "the harmony of the universe" (a positively valued state of affairs among the Navaho) and "individual independence" (a positively valued state among the Texans). A similar tradition has been maintained in the development of the Parsonian calculus, also at Harvard, but the Parsonian schema has emphasized the classification of these already broad abstractions into a componential taxonomy of value types. (For instance, a society's central values may be simply classified as "universalistic-achievement," or "particularistic-ascription," in character; cf., Parsons and Shils, 1952). This kind of typology has a certain usefulness as a heuristic device; its justification as an analytical tool we shall discuss later.

The term *ethos* denotes one particular kind of "object" to which value is apt to be commonly attached by members of a society. That "object" is style of emotional experience, or as Honigmann (1954) puts it, "the emotional quality of socially patterned behavior." The best-known example of the description of ethos is Ruth Benedict's famous *Patterns of Culture* (in which the word "pattern" is used to denote what we here call "ethos"). She contrasts two types of ethos, the Dionysian and the Apollonian (1934, p. 72):

> The desire of the Dionysian, in personal experience or in ritual, is to press through it toward a certain psychological state, to achieve excess. The closest analogy to the emotions he seeks is drunkenness, and he values the illuminations of frenzy. With Blake, he believes, "the path of excess leads to the palace of wisdom." The Apollonian distrusts all this, and has

often little idea of the nature of such experiences. He
finds means to outlaw them from his conscious life.
He "knows but one law, measure in the Hellenic
sense." He keeps the middle of the road, stays within
the known map, does not meddle with disruptive psychological states. In Nietzsche's fine phrase, even in
the exaltation of the dance he "remains what he is,
and retains his civic name."

Other writers have dealt with such culturally valued and
disvalued emotional states under a variety of terms:
thus, for instance, Belo (1935) has alluded to the
Balinese "temper," and Klineberg (1938) has reviewed
attitudes toward emotion expressed in Chinese literature.

The concept of *themes* in culture, as developed by,
among others, Morris Opler (1945), is also a value-
oriented concept. The themes of a culture are a finite
list (a dozen, let us say) of propositions about what constitutes the good life, about what are the valid and enduring goals of a human existence, shared by the members
of a group. In restricted form, thematic analysis has
been extensively used in the study of literary productions: novels, plays, movies, myths, and artificial productions, such as the Thematic Apperception Test. Such
themes describe, essentially, the familiar plots of a culture: those goals, positive and negative, together with
their methods of achievement and avoidance, which are
publicly recognized and intelligible to the audience
(Mead and Metraux, 1953). Thus, one can discern in
the popular American "Western," whether short story,
novel, movie, or television play, one ubiquitous theme:
the proposition that good men, hard to find in this
chaotic and lawless world, must fight and fight tirelessly
against great odds to bring order to the community, but
are sure to triumph and to receive sexual love and

public approbation, if not material reward, if they do. This theme is also dominant in the "tough" genre of crime stories, where the "private eyes" are typically disillusioned idealists, lacking faith in the power structure of their society, who nonetheless do the right thing for their wronged clients. The Western and private-eye themes are different from the late nineteenth-century English "mystery," whose heroes emphasized the virtue of cleverness in logical deduction, rather than of well-intentioned brutality, accepted the rightness of the power structure, and tirelessly and politely worked to maintain order in an already well-ordered community. All three differ from the theme of the seventeenth-century English drama whose heroes are not concerned with the welfare of society, but with the gratification of private appetites in a community which is recognized to be hypocritical, corrupt, and exploitative.

Fundamentally, all the approaches that emphasize values—value studies per se, ethos, themes—postulate, in the mazeway of the individual, the existence of certain semantic parameters. One or the other of these parameters gives connotation to virtually all experience, but does not necessarily enter into the *explicit* definition of anything. They are the emotional counterparts of the semantic geometry and of the world view of a people. Every motive can theoretically be classified under the heading of one or another value or theme, but the identity of these values is apt to emerge only after extensive coding and super-coding of the data of culture and of individual behavior.

NATIONAL CHARACTER AND BASIC PERSONALITY

THE DESCRIPTION OF the national character of a people is apt to include statements about genius, world view, and values. What distinguishes national character as a concept is, first, its usual restriction to the citizens of modern, politically organized states; and, second and more important, its emphasis upon the articulation of a large number of components into a structure or pattern. (Pattern, in this sense, does not quite mean the same thing as it does in Benedict's usage. Benedict's "patterns" were, essentially, simple emotional elements found in most of the units of a cultural structure, comparable to the chromosomes found in most of the cells of a body. But the "pattern" of a national character structure is a set of intricate dynamic interrelationships among different units of a personality or character.) The kind of phenomenon to which national character refers is the same as that denoted by the phrase "basic personality." But basic personality is applicable to any culturally bounded group, whether tribe, nation, or culture area; and it has tended to connote a more thoroughgoing use of the psychoanalytic theory of personality. It is inconvenient to have to change terms according to political form, however, and awkward to use the adjective "national" to refer to any and all social groups. So, in this section, we shall use the term "basic personality," in order to have one phrase, whether the group be a small primitive tribe, a modern state, a culture area, or a whole civilization. In this usage, we also disavow partiality to any particular theoretical schema. Thus, basic personality, as we shall use the term, implies neither a particular type of social organization nor a particular theory of personality; it merely refers to a structure of articulated personality characteristics and processes attributable, non-statistically, to almost all members of some culturally bounded population.

In method, the basic personality approach primarily rests on the cultural deductive principle; that is to say, the analyst first prepares an ethnographic description and then infers, from the ethnographic data, the intrapsychic structures of the members of the society (Mead, 1953; Wallace, 1952b). He feels able to do this because he is equipped with a complex, often psychoanalytic, theory which states equivalences between behavior (or experience) and motivation. Thus, knowledge of how children are toilet-trained, or how the dead are mourned, implies some knowledge of, respectively, consequent and antecedent motivational structures; this knowledge increases with the complexity of the description of the context of action. Furthermore, this theory requires the basic personality analyst to discriminate between peripheral and nuclear motives: nuclear motives are both "basic" to psychodynamic structure and "universal" in the society. The analyst is interested primarily in nuclear motives. The relationship of nuclear motives is, generally speaking, considered to form a conflict-structure, with motives (and values) being paired off against one another, dialectically, with overt behavior representing some sort of compromise synthesis. The basic motivational structure is assumed to be learned, usually in infancy and early childhood; later experience, however, and especially stressful experience, may lead to the development, or use, of various institutionalized mechanisms. These defend the essential integrity of the structure by giving indirect gratification to the subordinate but rebellious motives.

An example of basic personality theory is Gorer's controversial swaddling hypothesis. Geoffrey Gorer, in discussing the Great Russians, suggested that Russian culture institutionalized extreme discipline and authoritarianism in human relations, but allowed periods of orgiastic license for creature indulgence and for destructiveness. This seemed to imply (by the cultural deductive method) a type of personality in which the ego feels a need for strong external restraints in order to satisfy the value placed on discipline and order, and to control the rebellious desire for freedom from restraint. This conflict structure, in Gorer's theory, was established in the infant (but was reinforced in many other later experiences) by the experience of prolonged tight swaddling, with occasional intervals of release during which the child kicked violently, while nurses watched anxiously, fearful lest the child injure himself in his freedom (Gorer and Rickman, 1949; Mead and Metraux, 1953). As Mead points out, much of the criticism of Gorer's hypothesis is misdirected: Gorer did *not* say that Russians are incapable of freedom because they are swaddled as infants (Mead, 1953). Given the assumption that a common conflict structure exists in all Great Russians and that it is both the psychological equivalent of certain adult institutions and the product of certain series of infantile experiences, the hypothesis is rational. The appropriate criticism, if any, must apply to the assumptions.

This appropriate criticism is essentially that which applies to microcosmic theories in general. What is the evidence that all Great Russians do experience this conflict structure; that their adult institutions are the cultural equivalents of this uniform conflict structure; that their infantile experience is uniform; that their infantile experience determines their adult personalities? These questions anticipate further discussion; for the moment, however, we defer their consideration and go on to the closely related concept of modal personality.

MODAL PERSONALITY STRUCTURE

BASIC PERSONALITY is a non-statistical concept, emphasizing the importance of pattern and attempting to dispose of questions of frequency by excluding "deviants" and "peripheral" traits, thus leaving a core structure which is supposedly common to all members of a group. The corresponding statistical construct is modal personality. Properly speaking, "modal" refers to that value of a variable which is most frequent in a distribution: it is conceptually, and often empirically, distinct from other measures of central tendency, such as the mean (average) and the median. But for simplicity's sake, in the following section we shall use "modal personality" loosely to denote any method which characterizes the personality typical of a culturally bounded population by the central tendency of a defined frequency distribution.

Cultural descriptions rarely are phrased in such a way that statistical distributions of personal characteristics can be deduced from them. Hence modal personality must, in most cases, be constructed from data other than an ethnographic report. Such data are most easily gathered by giving psychological tests to a sample of a culturally defined population; other devices, such as recording dreams, taking life histories, and recording the frequency of certain behaviors, are sometimes used, but they are more tedious and consequently more difficult to apply to adequately large numbers of people. Thus, modal personality has come to be associated with the various projective techniques: the Rorschach Test, the Thematic Apperception Test (both in its original form and in the various cultural modifications), the Stewart

Emotional Response Test, and a number of others. There exists a considerable literature now on the cross-cultural use of projective techniques (cf., Henry and Spiro, 1953).

The peculiar weakness of the modal personality concept is complementary to the weakness of the basic personality concept. Basic personality has difficulty dealing with questions of frequency; modal personality has difficulty dealing with questions of structure and pattern. As we have seen, the basic personality theory uses the relationship of conflict to bind motives into elaborate homeostatic systems which are transformed over time, shifting and moving according to the pressures put upon them. Modal personality description can do as little as stating the central tendency of a frequency distribution of values of one variable, and must content itself at best with stating the frequency of certain combinations of values on several variables. Thus, for instance, Wallace was able to state that the modal type of personality, defined on twenty-one dimensions of observation in a certain Indian population, was shared by only 37 per cent of the sample tested (Wallace, 1952a). Such combinations, whether identified by simple techniques of correlation and association, or by factor analysis, or by the modal group technique described by Wallace (1952a), in themselves do not constitute a dynamic structure; they are essentially taxonomic structures. The dynamic structure (e.g., the conflict structure) represented by a particular combination of values (e.g., a Rorschach profile) must be deduced from a formal interpretive code. Furthermore, many modal personality studies are vulnerable to statistical criticism of sample design, of choice of statistic, and of the justification of inference. A further corollary weakness of the statistical approach is that the method requires extreme selectivity.

The richness of human experience is not savored, for the choice of a statistical tool usually means that only a few dimensions of behavior can be tapped and that these must be integrated into aridly abstract types.

Nevertheless, a statistical approach has the great virtue of making it possible (despite the common error of treating central tendencies as if they represented all the individual instances) to recognize the diversity of human characteristics within culturally bounded groups like tribes, nations, sex, age, status, class groups, and so on. It is upon the notion of the organization of diversities, as well as the reproduction of uniformity, that a progressive science of human behavior must base itself.

DIACHRONIC DISTRIBUTIONS

CHILD DEVELOPMENT

THE MOST CONVENTIONAL time sequence in culture-and-personality is the transformation of a cohort of asocial infants into socialized adults. The special assumption usually made here is that the transformation of any cohort is accomplished by its manipulation at the hands of a preceding cohort which has undergone the same transformation. Gorer (in Mead and Metraux, 1953, p. 63) has stated it clearly:

> It is on the basis of social continuity that the assumption is made that in any given society (or portion of society, where the society is large enough to be differentiated by regions or classes or a combination of both) the observable adults shared experiences and vicissitudes of childhood similar to those which observable infants and children are now undergoing; and further, that observable infants and children will

grow up to have shared predispositions and characters
similar to those of the observable adults. This assumption of *recapitulation* would seem to be the basic
assumption of the study of national character, and is
the assumption that divides the study of national character from the study of individual psychology.

This model of continuous intergenerational transformation, since it makes of each cohort a replica of its adult
predecessor, is logically comparable to models of genetic
copying in biological reproduction. The mechanism, in
genetics, is the gene, which carries genetic information
to each cell of the maturing organism, instructing it how
to respond to various circumstances. National character,
in Gorer's sense, is the analogue of genetic structure in
the geneticist's sense: it is assumed to be constant for
each "cell" in the social organism, and to carry the
information which determines the response of that
"cell" to its environment. It is this analogy which rationalizes Mead's assertion which has already been mentioned with some disapproval earlier in this chapter:

> Any member of a group, provided that his position
> within that group is properly specified, is a perfect
> sample of the group-wide pattern on which he is acting
> as an informant. So a twenty-one-year-old boy born
> of Chinese-American parents in a small upstate New
> York town who has just graduated *summa cum laude*
> from Harvard and a tenth-generation Boston-born
> deaf mute of United Kingdom stock are equally per-
> fect examples of American national character, *pro-
> vided that their individual position and individual
> characteristics are taken fully into account* (1953, p.
> 648).

Mead is asserting that the differences between the Chi-
nese-American and the Boston-born deaf mute are of
the same order as the differences between a neurone in
a person's brain and an epithelial cell in the same per-

son's finger: each is (in the analogy) a perfect mature expression of the same genetic structure developing under different circumstances. A result of phrasing the problem of temporal sequence in this genetic form is that two socialization processes may be considered. One is the process by which the "genotype"—the cultural character and the basic personality—is transmitted from one generation to the next; the other is the process by which individuals are "phenotypically" differentiated from one another, as the result of differential experience, in order to play different social roles.

Anthropologists always have been interested in the techniques used in the education (or "enculturation" or "socialization") of the young in a given socio-cultural system. In part, this interest is inseparable from the task of general ethnography. Thus, for instance, it has long been recognized that much of the ritual impedimenta of society is devoted to the task of accomplishing, with maximum speed, the social and psychological transformation of individuals. Many *rites de passage* explicitly aim at effecting in individuals certain changes in motivation, appropriate to the newly assumed social roles which are publicly proclaimed by the ritual. Ceremonies at puberty ("initiation rites"), at marriage, at entrance into organizations, at bereavement, and so on, have the dual function of notifying society of the change in role and of instilling in the participants the values and beliefs which will make performance of the new role congenial. A few anthropologists have been interested in the sequential structure of conditioning processes whose role transitions are discontinuous. They have suggested, for instance, that without such ritual conditioning the individual pays a "great psychic cost" (Benedict, 1938). But it is not known, in general, how effective *rites de passage* of various kinds are, under various circumstances, in accomplishing the motivational transformation of the individual. Similarly, although a few anthropologists have interested themselves in primitive methods of "formal" education (e.g., Pettitt, 1946), an analysis of the efficiency of these procedures is lacking.

Studies emphasizing developmental processes within the "family" (which, of course, is not the same thing from one society to the next) largely have been guided by culturally modified psychoanalytic hypotheses. Whiting's group at Harvard, in their cross-cultural survey of child-rearing practices and various cultural variables, seeks statistically reliable correlations between developmental experience and adult institutionalized behavior (Whiting and Child, 1953). Mead and her associates, in their less statistically organized studies, have described patiently how the multiple and unfolding experience of the child gradually induces an adult who plays (more or less) the same culturally standardized roles as his parents did before him. In this kind of work, as we have pointed out earlier, the facts of individual diversity and of culture change are held constant conceptually; the system is treated as if uniformity, synchronically and diachronically, were the rule (Mead, 1947b). Despite the consequent deficiencies, which we have already labored to disclose, an impressive consequence of such studies of age patterning is the demonstration of the fact of multiple imprinting of a relatively small number of broad themes or values, each with its special phrasing for various age, sex, and other conditions, by the immensely complex sequential pattern of experiences to which the growing person is subjected in any organized society. This process may not be as reliable as is believed, but the *kind* of process is well authenticated. As Mead (1947b, p. 634) eloquently observes:

. . . *simultaneity of impact* is carried not only by the behavior of each individual with whom the child comes in contact, but is also mediated by ritual, drama, and the arts. The shape of a pot, the design on the temple door, the pattern of the courtyard, the form of the bed, the grave posts or the funeral urn, the dancer's headdress and the clown's mask, are again reinforcements and whole statements of the same pattern which the child is experiencing serially.

It is worth remarking that, despite the ceremonial deference shown to academic psychology's learning theories in anthropological research, the kind of learning that goes on in patterning by multiple imprinting is not adequately described by formal learning theory. Consequently, efforts (like that of Whiting's, reported in *Becoming a Kwoma,* 1941) to use learning theory to analyze the socialization process, or language learning, do not evoke the more complex psychological reality which Mead's poetic language calls forth (cf., Chomsky, 1959). Possibly, models of learning by "imprinting," which follows the "law of effort" (cf., Hess, 1959), will prove to be more useful to anthropologists in analyzing the enculturation process than current reinforcement theory which emphasizes the "law of effect."

Wallace (1952b), in an effort to rehabilitate the notion of individual differences, formulated a probabilistic statement of the relation between cultural learning and personality development:

. . . the probability of any definable sequence of formative events is equal to the probability of the emergence of a given type of personality, and the total number of individuals possessing that type of personality will be the product of that probability and the size of the population.

But Wallace's formulation, like Sapir's and Spiro's cited earlier, still leaves unresolved the basic problem of all these procedures: the reliability of the processes *as they are operationally defined.*

Most treatments of child development processes seem to imply either that development is a very reliable process which can be predicted from a knowledge of cultural milieu and family situation, or that it is a very unreliable process. The proponents of reliability include most of, if not all, the child development workers in culture-and-personality. But some disquieting reports exist in the psychological and sociological literature which, taken at face value, suggest that cherished assumptions about supposedly invariant relations between infantile experience and adult personality are not verifiable by rigorous investigation (Orlansky, 1949; Sewell, 1952). Proponents of reliability may point out, in defense, that rigorous studies which attempt to "control" all but a few factors simply abolish the phenomenon under investigation. The solution of this problem can only be found by abandoning the expectation that *any* study will in the near future be able to demonstrate near-perfect reliability for developmental processes, not because the processes are not lawful, but because they are so fantastically complex and so protracted that empirical observation cannot record a sufficient number of relevant dimensions. This, however, is the standard situation at any scientific frontier. Progress now can be made by discovering empirically what the limits of confidence are in predictions of personality development. Such limits presumably will vary, both with the complexity and identity of the particular aspect of the developmental process being predicted, and with the number and identity of independent variables on which the prediction is based. Cross-cultural research into the differential reliability of developmental disciplines will pay handsome dividends, both in practical knowledge and in advancing knowledge of culture and personality as related systems.

INTERGENERATIONAL CHANGE IN GROUP CHARACTER

THE REPLICATION-OF-UNIFORMITY approach does not, in itself, allow for intergenerational change; it simply assumes that the *same* pattern is transmitted from generation to generation. Students of culture-and-personality do, nevertheless, recognize that group character changes over time (although, it has been suggested, basic personality is apt to lag behind cultural change). The mechanism for an intergenerational change in replication theory must be a variation in the manner in which a new cohort is treated by the older generation. What processes can induce such change in adult behavior? Some of the answers are extremely cautious. Mead (1953, p. 647), for instance, in her review of the theoretical position of workers in the field of national character, merely observes *apropos* of culture change:

> Each culture may be expected to change concomitantly with impinging events which were hitherto outside the system—an invasion from a hitherto unknown people, an earthquake, an epidemic arising outside the society, and so on. . . .

She also nods in passing to the concept of cultures as "historically patterned systems," and notes that "each member of each generation, from infancy to old age, contributes to the . . . reinterpretation of the cultural forms." Conversely, ill-advised adventures in culture change may collapse when they collide with the national character of a people (Mead, 1953, p. 647). Such relations between intergenerational changes in personality and cultural events outside the maturational cycle is, presumably, mediated by the child development process itself. Economic and technological changes, for instance, which occur as the result of rational ("peripheral") motives or of coercive environmental changes, may set in motion other changes which ultimately bring about alterations in child-rearing practices. Thus, intergenerational change in character can come about via cultural changes which first affect *post*-infantile experience. Riesman, for instance (1950), sees a general relationship between demographic condition, economic process, family structure, and personality structure. In almost all such studies, personality is conceived as the dependent variable and economic change (or migration) as the independent, with socialization practices as an intervening variable, dependent on economic change (or migration). Changes in basic personality, furthermore, are usually granted to be very slow and to become noticeable only after efforts to restrain or channel culture change have failed, and after the basic personality has suffered gross and painful distortion under stress.

Cultural changes which increase the heterogeneity of the society, such as acculturation and urbanization, often are believed to pose a serious threat to both personality and social integration (cf., Mead, 1947b; Beaglehole, 1949). The notion that heterogeneous cultures, split into incongruous fragments, must inevitably produce conflict-ridden personalities, is a corollary of the common-motive thesis which defines integration as a function of homogeneity. From the organization-of-diversity standpoint, however, culture change is not necessarily traumatic; indeed, it is to be regarded as the natural condition of man. If we regard most "living" cultures as heterogeneous and in constant, relatively rapid change (rapid change, incidentally, does not necessarily imply either change in material artifacts or rapid cumulative evolution), we note first that heterogeneity and change by definition no longer imply psychological and cultural disorganization. The causes of such disorganization must be sought elsewhere than in heterogeneity and change per se. The fundamental problem again becomes the organization of diversity rather than the replication of uniformity.

Now it is possible that when the culture is "heterogeneous" and rapidly changing, there will be a wider variety of personality types produced than in the homogeneous, slowly changing culture. Each of these types may be as consistent internally as any type produced in a stable homogeneous culture. The problem of such a complex society will not be that all of its members have split personalities, but rather that the problems of sociocultural organization may exceed the capacities of its members. Under the latter eventuality, many individuals secondarily may experience privation and frustration and come to suffer from psychosomatic and neurotic complaints; but these will be the consequence of failure of the system to answer the wants of certain of its members. This leads, in turn, to the suspicion that the traditionally disadvantaged sub-groups in a society—e.g., ethnic or religious minorities, native populations under foreign domination, and the lower economic classes— may suffer high incidences of discomfort and illness. This is not directly because of the heterogeneity of the society, but because of the particular disadvantages from which they happen to suffer disproportionately, such as inadequate nutrition, contempt, epidemic illness, physical abuse, and (as we shall discuss in more detail in the following chapter) the shock of cultural loss.

[I V]

The Psychology of Culture Change

IN THIS CHAPTER we shall take up in more detail the subject of how psychological processes affect, and are affected by, changes in culture. The reader should keep in mind, throughout the discussion, the conceptual distinction between affective and cognitive components of motivation. Derivative from this distinction is a corollary: the distinction between emotions and values. And the reader must keep in mind that two sorts of values are inherent in any motivational structure: consummatory values ("wants") and instrumental values ("needs").

INNOVATION: THE PROCESS OF INVENTION AND DISCOVERY

THERE IS AN OLD ADAGE to the effect that "there is nothing new under the sun." This piece of folk wisdom is quoted when some innovation is discovered to have had a prototype in an ancient or exotic community; it is intended as a reproach to the pride of latter-day innovators. But behind the seeming paradox (for we "know" that innovations occur) lie two significant problems.

The first is that some societies—in particular, the ancient Near Eastern societies from which our own culture has been derived—have defined apparent innovations not as "new" things, but merely as stages in a repetitive cosmic cycle. In such a view, a "new" technological device or a "revolutionary" social transformation is no more an innovation than is the coming of spring or the eruption of a baby's first tooth; such changes in state are merely stages in a recurrent process. Thus, our modern notion of an innovation as a *new identity* is, to a degree, culturally determined, and our very willingness to think of innovations is a habit of thought distinctive of ourselves.

The second problem, foreshadowed by the first, is the philosophical problem of identity. What are the criteria by which we do, or should, decide, that two perceptual experiences were stimulated by the same phenomenon? When are we, or should we be, content to say that a thing no longer exists, or that a new thing has come into existence? The answers to these questions are important not merely as observations on the psychological processes of innovation itself; they also will affect the manner in which innovation is investigated.

Homer Barnett (1953), the author of the most extensive anthropological treatise on the subject of innovation, devotes a large part of his volume to the philosophical analysis of identity and to the psychological processes by which it is recognized. Barnett takes issue with those older psychologists who claim that the organization of perception is dependent on the formal properties of the *thing* observed. In pointing out that much of perception is determined by the past experience of the perceiver, he is in the more contemporary perceptual psychologist's tradition; and, incidentally, in conformity with the viewpoint expressed by Hallowell (1955) concerning the dependence of perception on culturally predictable experience. This quasi-independence of perception from the "objective" reality of nature makes possible two mental phenomena: first, the ability of the perceiver to say that two sensibly different experiences involve the "same thing" ("sameness" being determined by constancy of configuration, by continuity over time in space, or by various other criteria); second, the possibility of two perceivers, or the same observer at different times, perceiving the "same" object differently, depending on differences in their own perceptual equipment and experience. The former ability makes possible learning and cultural continuity; but the latter makes possible culture change. "The mental interaction between what is and what was, in fact, does provide the only basis for a recombination of natural events; that is, for innovation, the uniquely mental contribution to newness" (Barnett, 1953, p. 448).

Barnett goes on to analyze the logical structure of innovation in such a way as to avoid, in part, the dilemma of developmentalism vs. discontinuity. Innovation is conceived as entirely a mental process and its substance as not "things" but "mental configurations" (i.e., "any unified pattern[s] of experience"). Every innovation (or discovery) is essentially a recombination of two or more mental configurations. The innovator does three things to these configurations: (1) he analyzes each of them, discriminating their component elements and considering the relations among these elements; (2) he matches them, identifying certain elements of one with certain elements of another, in the context provided by the particular configurations; (3) he recombines the configurations, substituting the identified elements and recognizing changes in the mutual relations among the several elements. The process may be very simply exemplified in the following paradigm, in which verbal statements are taken as the prototype and the stimulus configurations of interest and as the innovative idea (innovative, that is, in the context of these statements):

Stage 1 (Analysis)
Prototype: "Submarines, with a submarine shape, move slowly in relation to their length."
Stimulus: "Fish, with a fish shape, swim fast in relation to their length."

Stage 2 (Identification)
Identify "fish" with "submarine."
Identify "swim" with "move."
Identify "fish shape" with "submarine shape."

Stage 3 (Recombination)
Substitute "fish shape" for "submarine shape" in prototype statement.
Substitute "fast" for "slowly" in prototype statement.
Innovative statement: "Submarines, with a fish shape, move fast in relation to their length."

The innovative statement (a valid one, incidentally) is a new configuration, and a new *Gestalt,* with all sorts of implications for submarine design, naval strategy, and so forth; but, as Barnett argues, no element or relation is uniquely new, since the morphemes and syntax were both provided by the prior statements.

The "recombination of configurations" thesis has the virtue of answering the question of where the pieces come from, and thereby aligns the analysis of the innovative process with the study of other natural processes,

in which the "new" state of any system is a function of
the "old." But while this eliminates the problem of discontinuity, it exacerbates the complementary problem
of continuity. Every innovation, and thus all culture
change, must be considered to be a recombination of
previously existing configurations. This makes any evolutionary sequence in culture comparable to the development of the logical implications of a set of axiomatic
propositions, and suggests that a "beginning" must exist
where one could find certain primitive configurations
from which all subsequent recombinations have been
derived. This, however, is precisely Bastian's notion of
Elementargedanken, which has proved to be an inadequate foundation for studies of cultural evolution and
also for inquiries into the nature of the psychic unity of
man (cf., Wallace, 1961). A further implication of the
recombination thesis is that there exists a finite, even if
very large, number of possible configurations, the magnitude of this number being determined by the size of
the original set of elements and relations. This, in turn,
requires the deduction that there is a finite number of
possible cultures.

The partial inadequacy of the recombination thesis,
however, lies not in any necessary fallacy of the assertion that every innovation is a recombination of pre-
existing mental configurations (even though the implications of this position are so far-reaching, as to be
untestable and hence metaphysical). It lies, rather, in
the inadequacy of the position to state the conditions
under which a particular innovation will occur; i.e., to
predict which of several possible recombinations will
be made, by whom, and when. Predictions of this sort
involve considerations of personal motivation, idiosyncratic experience, cultural and situational milieu, and
general cognitive process.

Motivational theories of innovative behavior are of two kinds: (1) "positive" theories which attempt to account for the creative act; (2) "negative" theories which attempt to account for non-innovative conservatism. These theories vary widely with respect to their level of generality, some applying to all organisms which can learn, and others applying only to specific subgroups in particular human societies (e.g., to professional inventors in twentieth-century America). Perhaps the most generalized positive motivation theory is that which postulates an instinct or drive, characteristic of all organisms, to explore, to play, to experience and satisfy "curiosity," to enjoy aesthetic pleasure, to reduce the "cognitive dissonance" between imagination and reality (Linton, 1936; Festinger, 1957). Wallace (1961) has formulated this postulate in terms of organization theory:

> [The] Principle of Maximal Organization . . . asserts that an organism acts in such a way as to maximize, under existing conditions, and to the extent of its capacity, the amount of organization in the dynamic system represented in its mazeway; that is to say, it works to increase both the complexity and the orderliness of its experience.

When circumstances are such that a particular innovative recombination will maximize the organization quantity in a given mazeway, and the physiological milieu is adequate to support the cognitive task, then that innovation will be produced (cf., Wallace, 1956a and 1956b). Such a recombination will not, however, occur unless the necessary prototypical and stimulus configurations are already present.

Another body of theory takes up the problem of the processes by which the prototype and stimulus configurations necessary for a particular innovation are assembled in a mazeway. White (1949), Kroeber (1944), and many others (including a number of historians and sociologists), disputing the popular impression that genius spontaneously creates a cultural something out of an idiosyncratic nothing, have presented evidence to show that particular innovations are apt to be independently and almost simultaneously produced by many individuals in a given type of cultural milieu. Such instances of simultaneous invention suggest strongly that culture, as it evolves, "provides" many individuals with the prototype and stimulus configurations necessary to a given innovation, and that only certain innovations are possible in any given cultural milieu.

What can one say about the psychological properties, including the motivations, of the innovators? First of all, it is virtually necessary to assume, as Barnett does, and as organization theory implies, that all persons occasionally innovate within the limits imposed by their own culture, local situation, and individual abilities. Some innovation occurs by chance and by cognitive error. Furthermore, societies may be congenial or uncongenial to innovation, depending on the cognitive process by which the innovation was accomplished. Thus, for instance, seventeenth-century Iroquois culture highly encouraged religious (ritual and mythological), political, and even economic innovation if the cognitive modality was hallucinatory (Wallace, 1958b). In our own society, scientific, technological, religious, and artistic innovation is readily rewarded, irrespective of the cognitive modality by which it is achieved, but political and economic innovation is far less so, and has virtually no chance of success if the cognitive modality of discovery is known to be hallucinatory. If one approaches the matter of motivation from the standpoint of reinforcement learning theory, one would expect that members of a society will "learn" to innovate in precisely those cultural areas in which innovation is apt to be rewarded by the society (or, at least, his part of it). These are the areas, to use Herskovits' (1948) phrase, of "cultural focus." In such areas, the drive for maximal organization is most apt to find satisfaction. But it would be a mistake to carry such a faith in the cultural conformity of innovation too far, for here we are dealing as much or more with the criteria of acceptance as with the process of innovation. As we have suggested, innovation may reap rewards other than those society offers. Creativity is notoriously difficult either to command or to suppress. Innovation, indeed, seems to be produced by a most extraordinarily heterogeneous population, under the most remarkably varied circumstances, and for such highly diversified conscious purposes that one suspects that innovation, per se, as a mental process, is almost independent of motivation; in itself innovation is an "instinctive" propensity of the human organism, activated under the merest provocation of desire for richer or more orderly experience. It is more likely that motivational processes of the kind connoted by the term "personality" will govern *response* to innovation (including the innovator's own response).

RESPONSE TO INNOVATION: ACCEPTANCE, USE, AND REJECTION

ANTHROPOLOGISTS TRADITIONALLY have maintained interest in those psychological processes which determine whether a proposed innovation will be accepted or rejected for use by the innovator himself, by other mem-

bers of his society, and (in diffusion and acculturation
situations) by members of other societies. In such situations, typically, the innovation is conceived as being
any configuration, new to a culture, which is presented
by an agent of change, such as an inventor, a trader, a
religious or political reformer, a war prisoner, or a
spouse from an alien cultural setting. Such an offered
innovation may be conceived as a stimulus configuration
which is matched with a prototype maintained by the
recipient. Acceptance of the innovation thus will result,
usually, in its modification in order that it may fit into
the larger cultural *Gestalt,* but for the sake of simplicity
we shall speak of "acceptance" without mentioning the
modification process explicitly. The members of the
community consider the innovation, accept or reject it,
and finally (if it is accepted) use it. (Obviously, we are
not here considering such micro-innovations as are involved in linguistic drift, which do not seem to involve
rational evaluation.) These processes need not be
deliberate or even conscious: the only necessary assumption is that the innovation must pass through a sort of
screen, which evaluates it as a "new thing," before any
substantial use can be made of it.

The acculturation situation generally conforms well
to the model described above: a "donor" culture "presents" a "new" cultural configuration to the "recipient"
culture. The members of this culture then subject the
new configuration to various tests and, sooner or later,
accept or reject it. The mechanisms involved, however
poorly understood, have come to be of major practical
importance in the modern world as, both internally and
externally, the various national governments anxiously
strive to induce potential allies, as well as their own
people, to undertake new patterns of culture.

One kind of determinant is the so-called "psychological screen" which modal personality structure interposes between presentation and acceptance. This screen sorts presented innovations into two groups: (1) those which are compatible with some structure of motives common in the society; (2) those which are not. The motivational structure connoted in this process exists on a high level of abstraction, consisting of broad values implicit in ethos, national character, or modal personality structure, such as the desirability of material wealth, or the relative importance of kinship and community obligations, the definition of masculinity, or the significance of punctuality (cf., Wallace, 1951; Linton, 1947). Any single affectively-weighted category of this kind can be used to classify a large number of particular innovations which would seem to be immediately relevant to more limited contexts. Thus, these values function as constant parameters of choice in a culture, giving connotation to most phenomena, however disparate their individual definitions. It may be noted that the psychologist Osgood's (1957) semantic testing device (the "semantic differential") is eminently suited for use in assessing the function of such broad values in giving connotative values to a variety of existential phenomena, including innovative proposals.

If an innovation succeeds in passing the screen of general values, however, it faces still other tests. (The reader will note, of course, that the order of these discrimination functions is chosen for heuristic purposes and does not necessarily exist in nature.) Certain of these other obstacles to acceptance constitute together the major part of the concern of "applied" and "action" anthropology. Their general character is "functional": that is to say, the criterion of acceptability is the conviction, on the part of potential recipients, that the innovation will, in sum, contribute more importantly to the satisfaction of a network of wants and needs than to their frustration. Once an innovation acquires such a cultural meaning, it has itself the status of a felt need. It is necessary to point out, of course, that the donor's conception of the wants and needs of the recipients is not necessarily the same as the recipient's own conception. There now exists a sizable body of literature in applied anthropology, describing and analyzing situations wherein potential recipients refused to accept innovations which donors expected them to embrace warmly. The error of the donor generally lies in neglecting to assess the relevant negative functions of the proposed innovation; that is to say, in incorrectly identifying the institutionalized motives which the innovation would actually tend to frustrate (cf., Goodenough, n.d.; Paul, 1955; Mead, 1955; Spicer, 1952).

A further obstacle to the acceptance of innovations, in most recipient societies, is the existence of groups with different vested interests, grievances, or ambitions. American anthropology, because of its tendency (abetted in part by the earlier culture-and-personality school) to concentrate attention on behavioral homogeneity, even in complex societies, has had some difficulty in coming to grips with intra-societal groups. British social anthropology, with its emphasis on the interaction between social entities, such as kin groups, corporations, and the like, has sometimes seemed to Americans to neglect "psychological" processes. Continental scholarship goes even farther: building on a century's tradition of intense interest in the conflict of interest groups, particularly the social classes, the European social scientist seems to be living in a world of mystically abstract intergroup dynamics, wherein social classes collide, plot, and counter-plot, like vast shadows on a giant screen. But it is of the utmost importance to the theory of culture and personality that anthropologists incorporate, and use, British and European insights into the dynamic role of group loyalties, identifications, and interests, in determining the course of culture change. The fact that systematic group differentials, with respect to acculturation, can be shown to exist, even within small societies (cf., Spindler, 1955) is, of course, an important first step. It is also useful to point out, as applied anthropology has frequently done, that the vested interests of one individual or group may be jeopardized by an innovation which promotes the welfare of another; the consequence is apt to be rejection by one, acceptance by the other, and mutually destructive conflict between the two (sometimes displaced onto the donor). But the issues go beyond this commonly observed polarization of a society into more, or less, vigorously "pro-" and "anti-" factions with respect to any proposed innovation. The major point is that many societies, especially the more complex ones, are apt to maintain for considerable periods of time *two* major constellations of interest groups, irrespective of any innovation proffered from without. These two groups are termed by Karl Mannheim (a sociologist whose method of analysis is essentially anthropological) the proponents of *ideology* and the proponents of *utopia*. Ideology is the conservative world-view which rationalizes, expresses, and supports the existing socio-cultural system with which some members of the society are content. Utopia, on the other hand, is the revolutionary world-view which rationalizes, expresses, and supports efforts to transform the existing socio-cultural system in order to bring greater satisfaction to the discontented. In their mutual struggle, according to the traditional view of Mannheim's school, a synthesis of the two world-views will emerge to become the ideology of the dominant class in the next phase of the dialectical process (cf., Mannheim, 1936).

The importance for acculturation theory of such intra-societal struggles between ideology and utopia is that the response of the utopian mentality to a proposed innovation will *not* be based on considerations of its functional suitability in the existing socio-cultural system. Thus, the "utopian" response will differ from the response of the conservative, not merely by virtue of the different present behavioral systems of the two groups, but also by virtue of their different temporal orientation. The utopian's functional calculus will demand estimates of the innovation's utility in breaking up the existing system (i.e., on its negative value for his opponents) and on its virtue in the better world of the future. Thus, an innovation adroitly calculated to fit into an existing system with minimal disturbance may, paradoxically, be repudiated by the utopian faction, precisely because of its excellent adaptation to the current status quo. Another consequence of factionalism is that innovations, entirely apart from rationally calculated estimates of their functional value, may become symbols of social group membership. If that group membership is positively regarded, the innovation may be valued entirely out of proportion to its "intrinsic" worth; conversely, if its acceptance connotes identification with an "enemy" or "inferior" group, the individual who accepts it must abandon, or be abandoned by, the group to which he belongs. The individual's self-image and self-esteem are heavily dependent on his conception of his acceptability to the reference group with which he identifies himself; therefore, otherwise unimpeachable innovations, wherein acceptance implies identification with a negatively valued donor, may find acceptance difficult.

Having discussed various characteristics of the recipients, which affect the likelihood of acceptance or rejection of an innovation, we must now turn our attention to another group of factors. These factors are the various kinds and degrees of pressure which the donor may apply to the recipient, in the course of presentation, in order to ensure that the recipient accepts, or rejects, the innovation. It is rarely the case that the donor is indifferent to the recipient's response; usually, the donor has interests of his own which will be served by the recipient's acceptance or rejection of a given innovation. These donor interests are, as a group, extremely heterogeneous, ranging from honest concern for the welfare of the recipient society, through enlightened self-interest, to purely selfish purposes of an economic, military, or political character. Commonly, various donor motives are mixed, either in the same person or among various representatives of the donor. Furthermore, one donor may be concerned about ensuring rejection of another donor's "gifts": Quaker missionaries to the American Indians, for instance, worked hard to persuade their charges to reject such proffered innovations as whiskey, while they promoted the acceptance of the plow, the spinning wheel, and the loom.

The techniques employed by the donor generally involve presenting the innovation to the recipient under conditions suggesting that acceptance will be rewarding and non-compliance will be frustrating. In crude form, this means that the recipient either is openly bribed or threatened. In more subtle approaches, the donor's interests may be disguised and the reinforcement paradigm presented in such a way that the rewards do not appear to entail the sacrifice of other interests and the threats do not openly refer to any punitive action of the donor, but merely to an unwanted course of events. These events are inevitable under the circumstances and are irrespective of the donor's interests. American applied anthropology, as Goodenough (n.d.) emphasizes, is concerned with non-coercive "cooperation in change," which is ethically more attractive to most Americans and is often more effective. But an ethical preference for the non-coercive methods of free choice, of education and mutual aid, should not blind the theoretician to the fact that coercive methods frequently are employed by most societies, including our own, when methods of persuasion fail, because of the compelling motive which lies behind the donor's presentation. The history of religious wars, of political revolutions, of class, caste, and ethnic conflicts, of missionary enterprises, of public health and civil rights controversies, and of many other intergroup tensions, all testify to the readiness with which donor groups use more or less severely coercive measures to induce the acceptance of innovations, when recipient acceptance is viewed by the donor as necessary for the satisfaction of his own wants. The methods of coercion may be viewed as standing on a continuum of severity, from minimal to most severe. At the minimal pole, of course, stands the limiting case: presentation with indifference. Here the innovation may not have been intentionally presented at all; the recipient group has free choice to accept or to reject; response will be entirely determined by the values and the functional meaning of the innovation itself to the recipient society. Next stand the methods of peaceful example—persuasion, negotiation, and cooperation—analyzed by Goodenough (n.d.) at length. Here, the donor carefully attempts to develop a mutually beneficial relationship in change, in which the interests and motives of both parties are well satisfied on a long-term basis. A certain amount of peaceful argument and education may be offered by the donor, but no threat is implied or intended. More severe is the deliberate use of threat. Here, the formula is, in effect, "Accept (or reject) this innovation or you will be prevented from satisfying some want." Hellfire-and-damnation preachers, political overlords, and even friends and allies are apt to turn to this technique when less easy methods fail. This is also the device frequently employed by commercial advertisers attempting to induce a target group to accept its product: non-buyers are threatened with loss of friends, job, health, and sexual satisfaction, if they fail to buy the proffered soap, deodorant, toothpaste, liquor, hairdressing, perfume, or whatnot. Equally direct is the use of mass suggestion by entrapping the target population in a milieu in which they cannot escape the monotonous reiteration, in multiple channels and by multiple spokesmen, of the presentation. Such suggestion is notoriously effective in inducing mass acceptance of behaviors which, under circumstances of free choice, the component individuals would reject unhesitatingly. Finally, and most severe of all, is the use of techniques, such as physical torture and exhaustion, which produce in the target a psycho-physiological state wherein acceptance of innovation becomes almost automatic. Sargant (1957) sees in this process of conversion or "brain-washing" the operation of Pavlov's "paradoxical" and "ultra-paradoxical" modes of conditioning.

It is evident, in view of the considerations presented above, that prediction of group acceptance or rejection of an innovation, once presented, will be determined by the balance of a number of complexly interrelated psychological valences, negative and positive, in the individual mazeways of the group's members. The individual must, whether deliberately or not, calculate the sum of the organizational decrements and increments which acceptance will bring, and the sum of organizational dec-

rements and increments which rejection will bring. If
the sum total of all decrements and increments is positive, then the innovation will be accepted. The values
involved in such a calculation will, in the last analysis,
be personal (even though their distribution in the society
may be a cultural fact), and their evaluation by an outside observer will consequently be difficult. Nevertheless, knowledge of the screen of values imposed by ethos,
national character, or modal personality; of the functional structure of the present psychologically real culture of the population; of the vectors of nativism and
utopianism; and of the nature of the coercion (if any)
employed in presentation, will make it possible to form
a useful estimate of the likelihood of group acceptance.
Group acceptance or rejection, however, may be less
than uniform, because of the differential interests in the
innovation of the several sub-groups. Consequently, a
long process of intra-societal interaction, with one sub-
group attempting to influence others, is apt to ensue,
with each separate stage repeating the process described
above.

TYPES OF CULTURE CHANGE PROCESS

ANTHROPOLOGISTS TEND TO CONSIDER culture change
either over very long periods of time (macro-temporal
change), or over very brief periods of time (micro-temporal change). Macro-temporal processes are frequently
labeled cultural evolution and diffusion; micro-temporal
processes go by such rubrics as innovation, acculturation, and nativistic movement.

MACRO-TEMPORAL PROCESSES

STUDIES OF macro-temporal processes of culture change, covering hundreds or thousands of years, are generally based on the assumption that "human nature," whatever that is, must be treated as a constant parameter of cultural function and thus, for all practical purposes, may be ignored. The four major models share a common impersonality which is rarely broken by considerations, such as those of Eiseley (1958) and Angel (1960) of the human organism as a variable factor.

The Oscillation Model

CULTURALLY ORGANIZED SOCIETIES sometimes have been compared to organisms with a predisposing heredity and an evocative environment which pass through various stages of coming-into-being, maturation, maturity, senescence, and death. Various accidents along this path are treated as education, reproduction, trauma, illness, recovery, and so forth. While this historiographic use, like others, of the organismic analogy is vulnerable to criticism, nevertheless the model has inspired a number of scholars to undertake or interpret empirical studies, and thus it may be said to satisfy the minimal requirement of a good scientific model: to inspire research. The life-cycle model has particularly appealed to those humanistically inclined anthropologists, historians, and philosophers who have reflected on the rise, climax, and fall of the classic high civilizations; but, in principle, it is applicable to any society. The model typically implies a more or less complex oscillation of indices of cultural organization. Indeed, it is the notion of a more or less regular oscillation in level of cultural organization, over larger or smaller stretches of time, that is the important feature of this model; the organismic analogy is

merely a vehicle for the communication of the oscillation
idea.

The Partial-Ordering Evolution Model

NINETEENTH-CENTURY ETHNOLOGISTS believed that a
very large proportion of the data of ethnography could
be arranged in partial orderings which would represent
one evolutionary series. The term "unilinear evolution,"
applied to their theories, is derived from an implication
of the partial ordering model: that, in order for any society to change from one state to another, it must pass
successively through all the intervening points in the
scale of states. Thus, in such a model, societies in state
i must have passed through states $1, 2, \ldots, i\text{-}2, i\text{-}1$,
in that order. In this sense, their evolution has been
unilinear. Thus, Tylor (1900, pp. 20, 23-25) wrote:

> On the whole it appears that wherever there are found
> elaborate arts, abstruse knowledge, complex institu-
> tions, these are the results of gradual development
> from an earlier, simpler, and ruder life. No stage of
> civilization comes into existence spontaneously, but
> grows or is developed out of the stage before it. This
> is the great principle which every scholar must lay
> firm hold of, if he intends to understand either the
> world he lives in or the history of the past. . . . Hu-
> man life may be roughly classed into three great stages,
> Savage, Barbaric, Civilized. . . . So far as the evi-
> dence goes, it seems that civilization has actually
> grown up in the world in these three stages.

Tylor, in more detailed discussion, points out the bar-
baric and savage lineage not merely of civilization in
general, but of such specific civilized societies as Vic-
torian England and ancient Egypt and Babylonia. Although later, more relativistic anthropologists have realized that far fewer cultural elements scale, and that

many scale only under particular values of various parameters, such as ecological and culture area, the central notion of evolution, as a partial ordering correlated with time, has continued to receive recognition. In the more recent investigations of White and his colleagues (see particularly Sahlins and Service, 1960), significant qualifications of the unilinear viewpoint have been undertaken which meet many of the criticisms leveled at "evolutionism" in the past. A distinction is made between "special" evolution (the history of phylogenetic sequences) and "general" evolution (the partial ordering of first occurrences of major cultural innovations). The partial ordering of events in general evolution does not necessarily correspond to a partial ordering of events in any but *one* phylogenetic sequence; also, one phylogenetic sequence, because of the effectiveness of cultural diffusion, need not be (and in fact has not been) located within the boundaries of one social or geographical entity.

The Stochastic Evolution Model

IMPLICIT IN THE CONCEPT of partial ordering is the notion that a system in a given state i can change to one, and only one, next state j. This restriction makes the partial-ordering model perfectly predictive with respect to direction of change (though not with respect to whether or not change will occur). In some problems, however, it is not possible to justify such a rigid schema; one may wish only to state the probabilities of the system moving into alternative states $j_1, j_2, \ldots, j_m$, once it is in state i. Such probabilistic processes are exemplified by the evolution of kinship systems, as treated by Murdock (1949), and they can be conceptualized (although anthropologists do not conventionally do so) as the evolution of periodic and aperiodic stochastic (particularly Markov) processes. A stochastic process is a set of events so related that the probability of any one event occurring next in series is conditional upon the identity of the preceding event or events. Murdock demonstrates empirically, first of all, that certain significant statistical associations exist among the categories of social structure; i.e., some features of kinship entail others. Father's brother's daughter, for instance, tends to be referred to by the same term as wife's brother's wife in societies with exogamous moieties, but by a different term in societies without exogamous moieties. But these static associations are paralleled by dynamic associations in the form of rules stating the order in which three dimensions of social structure—rule of residence, type of descent, and type of kinship terminology—change, and stating the transition probabilities among the values on these dimensions. Furthermore, Murdock implicitly assumes that the rules are constant over long periods of time and thus that the process is "stationary." This, in turn, implies, via the ergodic hypothesis, that no matter what were the original frequencies of various types of social organization, these types gradually will assume a fairly fixed relative frequency among human cultures. The ergodic hypothesis asserts that, once a set of rules has been established, whatever the initial distribution of states, the universe of events more or less quickly (quickness depending on the rules of the statistical process and on the frequency of events of change) will approach a single asymptotic equilibrium distribution of states. One may, of course, question whether the "rules" which define the process are constant over any extended span of time; but, even with only temporary constancy of rule, the theory implies that great changes in the distribution of types of social organization may occur, on a world-wide scale, within a relatively brief span of time.

The Age-Area Diffusion Model

THE DIFFUSION of cultural content, with or without modification, from one society to another, when viewed on the grand scale sometimes can be conveniently conceptualized after the so-called age-area model. With respect to any trait, and often with respect to complexes, the data may be arranged on a map with a center of diffusion surrounded (in theory at least) by roughly concentric lines representing the limits of spread of the trait in question at successive time periods. It is apparent that the resulting concentric distribution is ordered (again, in fact, partially ordered) in such a way that the relative antiquity of the trait in an area is perfectly correlated with its rank order of geographic distance from the center of distribution.

This technique has been widely used in the analysis of data distributions by physical anthropologists, archaeologists, and ethnologists, for the reconstruction of extended historical processes and for the analysis of intergroup relations (as, for instance, in folk-urban differentials). At the present time, however, it is considerably less popular than evolutionary, directly historical, or micro-temporal models, because of the difficulty of analyzing the processes involved in the "diffusion" itself from purely cartographic syntheses (see Hodgen, 1952, pp. 116-121, for a critical discussion of the diffusion and age-area models).

MICRO-TEMPORAL PROCESSES

THE USE OF PERSONALISTIC CONSTRUCTS is more convenient in studies of change processes covering relatively brief spans of time, of the order of a few generations or less. Rather than attempt a complex typology, we shall consider only two categories: moving equilibrium processes and revitalization processes. These two types are relevant here because they can be derived from the psychological considerations introduced in the last section.

Moving Equilibrium Processes

A CULTURE, under certain conditions, during a period of time can be said to be an open system in a state of stable but moving equilibrium: that is to say, it maintains a boundary, accepts inputs and produces outputs at approximately equal rates, and changes continuously but gradually in internal structure. The inputs, in this case, are accepted innovations, acquired by invention, acculturation, or diffusion; the outputs, abandoned elements of culture. The quantity of organization of the system (the product of its complexity and its orderliness) remains relatively constant, or increases or decreases slowly.

Culture change during moving equilibrium has several characteristics, some of which we have discussed earlier in this chapter. First of all, the course of change appears as a chainlike series of acceptances and abandonments. The rate may be relatively fast or slow, and the changes themselves large or small; but the transformation of structure is accomplished by an orderly piece-by-piece replacement and realignment of parts. Because of the phenomenon of psychological screening and because of the structure of functional interests, there will be differentials in the susceptibility of various areas of culture to change. This will give rise to the phenomena of relatively frequent change within areas of so-called cultural focus, and of relatively infrequent change within areas of cultural lag. Furthermore, because of the existence of differential interest groups, in any society, responses to any given proposed innovation will differ. Very commonly, with respect to any given innovation, there will be a rejection and an acceptance faction. Those who generally favor innovations in "lag" areas of culture will be characterized as the radicals (utopians); those who resist innovation even in "focus" areas will be characterized as conservatives. Manifestly, the more complex the culture, the higher the likelihood of systematic intra-societal differentials in attitude toward proposed innovations, even under equilibrium conditions, and the more difficult the accomplishment of general acceptance of changes. These difficulties, in turn, can be considered to be the root problem of political organization in rapidly changing complex societies. Some sort of constitutional democratic political process and some sort of coordinated executive planning are both necessary to solve this problem: constitutional democratic process in order to ensure adequate communication, public confidence, and an acceptable balance of advantages and disadvantages for the various interest groups; and coordinated executive planning in order to prevent extreme and uncontrollable oscillations, unanticipated functional blockages, and undue slowness or randomness of change.

Revitalization Processes

IMPLICIT in the foregoing discussion was the assumption that, even during periods of stable moving equilibrium, the socio-cultural system is subject to mild but measurable oscillations in degree of organization. From time to time, however, most societies undergo more violent fluctuations in this regard. Such fluctuation is of peculiar importance in culture change because it often culminates in relatively sudden change in cultural *Gestalt*. We refer, here, to revitalization movements, which we define as deliberate, organized attempts by some members of a society to construct a more satisfying culture by rapid acceptance of a pattern of multiple innovations (see Wallace, 1956c; Mead, 1956).

The severe disorganization of a socio-cultural system may be caused by the impact of any one or combination of a variety of forces which push the system beyond the limits of equilibrium. Some of these forces are: climatic or faunal changes which destroy the economic basis of its existence; epidemic disease which grossly alters the population structure; wars which exhaust the society's resources of manpower or result in defeat or invasion; internal conflict among interest groups which results in extreme disadvantage for at least one group; and, very commonly, a position of perceived subordination and inferiority with respect to an adjacent society. The latter, by the use of more or less coercion (or even no coercion at all, as in situations where the mere example set by the dominant society raises too-high levels of aspiration), brings about uncoordinated cultural changes. Under conditions of disorganization, the system, from the standpoint of at least some of its members, is unable to make possible the reliable satisfaction of certain values which are held to be essential to continued well-being and self-respect. The mazeway of a culturally disillusioned person, accordingly, is an image of a world that is unpredictable, or barren in its simplicity, or both. His mood (depending on the precise nature of the disorganization) will be one of panic-stricken anxiety, shame, guilt, depression, or apathy.

An example of the kind of disorganization to which we refer is given by the two thousand or so Seneca Indians of New York at the close of the eighteenth century. Among these people, a supreme value attached to the conception of the absolutely free and autonomous individual, unconstrained by and indifferent to his own and others' pain and hardship. This individual was capable of free indulgence of emotional impulses but, in crisis, freely subordinated his own wishes to the needs of his community. Among the men, especially, this ego-ideal was central in personality organization. Men defined the roles of hunting, of warfare, and of statesmanship as the conditions of achievement of this value; thus, the stereotypes of "the good hunter," "the brave warrior," and "the forest statesman" were the images of masculine success. But the 43 years from 1754, when the French and Indian War began, to 1797, when the Seneca sold their last hunting grounds and became largely confined to tiny, isolated reservations, brought with them changes in their situation which made achievement of these ideals virtually impossible. The good hunter could no longer hunt: the game was scarce, and it was almost suicidally dangerous to stray far from the reservation among the numerous hostile white men. The brave warrior could no longer fight, being under-supplied, abandoned by his allies, and his women and children threatened by growing military might of the United States. The forest statesman was an object of contempt, and this disillusionment was perhaps more shattering than the rest. The Iroquois chiefs, for nearly a century, had been able to play off British and French, then Americans and British, against one another, extorting supplies and guarantees of territorial immunity from both sides. They had maintained an extensive system of alliances and hegemonies among surrounding tribal groups. Suddenly they were shorn of their power. White men no longer spoke of the League of the Iroquois with respect; their western Indian dependents and allies regarded them as cowards for having made peace with the Americans.

The initial Seneca response to the progress of sociocultural disorganization was quasi-pathological: many became drunkards; the fear of witches increased; squabbling factions were unable to achieve a common policy. But a revitalization movement developed in 1799, based on the religious revelations reported by one of the disillusioned forest statesman, one Handsome Lake, who preached a code of patterned religious and cultural reform. The drinking of whiskey was proscribed; witchcraft was to be stamped out; various outmoded rituals and prevalent sins were to be abandoned. In addition, various syncretic cultural reforms, amounting to a reorientation of the socio-economic system, were to be undertaken, including the adoption of agriculture (hitherto a feminine calling) by the men, and the focusing of kinship responsibilities within the nuclear family (rather than in the clan and lineage). The general acceptance of Handsome Lake's Code, within a few years, wrought seemingly miraculous changes. A group of sober, devout, partly literate, and technologically up-to-date farming communities suddenly replaced the demoralized slums in the wilderness.

Such dramatic transformations are, as a matter of historical fact, very common in human history, and probably have been the medium of as much culture change as the slower equilibrium processes. Furthermore, because they compress into such a short space of time such extensive changes in pattern, they are somewhat easier to record than the quiet serial changes during periods of equilibrium. In general, revitalization processes share a common process structure which can be conceptualized as a pattern of temporally overlapping, but functionally distinct, stages:

I. STEADY STATE   This is a period of moving equilibrium of the kind discussed in the preceding section. Culture change occurs during the steady state, but is of the relatively slow and chainlike kind. Stress levels vary among interest groups, and there is some oscillation in organization level, but disorganization and stress remain within limits tolerable to most individuals. Occasional incidents of intolerable stress may stimulate a limited "correction" of the system, but some incidence of individual ill-health and criminality are accepted as a price society must pay.

II. THE PERIOD OF INCREASED INDIVIDUAL STRESS
The socio-cultural system is being "pushed" progressively out of equilibrium by the forces described earlier: climatic and biotic change, epidemic disease, war and conquest, social subordination, acculturation, etc. Under these circumstances, increasingly large numbers of individuals are placed under what is to them intolerable stress by the failure of the system to accommodate the satisfaction of their needs. Anomie and disillusionment become widespread, as the culture is perceived to be disorganized and inadequate; crime and illness increase sharply in frequency as individualistic asocial responses. But the situation is still generally defined as one of fluctuation within the steady state.

III. THE PERIOD OF CULTURAL DISTORTION
Some members of the society attempt, piecemeal and ineffectively, to restore personal equilibrium by adopting socially disfunctional expedients. Alcoholism, venality in public officials, the "black market," breaches of sexual and kinship mores, hoarding, gambling for gain, "scape-goating," and similar behaviors which, in the preceding period, were still defined as individual deviancies, in effect become institutionalized efforts to circumvent the evil effects of "the system." Interest groups, losing confidence in the advantages of maintaining mutually acceptable interrelationships, may resort to violence in order to coerce others into unilaterally advantageous

behavior. Because of the mal-coordination of cultural changes during this period, they are rarely able to reduce the impact of the forces which have pushed the society out of equilibrium, and in fact lead to a continuous decline in organization.

IV. THE PERIOD OF REVITALIZATION   Once severe cultural distortion has occurred, the society can with difficulty return to steady state without the institution of a revitalization process. Without revitalization, indeed, the society is apt to disintegrate as a system: the population will either die off, splinter into autonomous groups, or be absorbed into another, more stable, society. Revitalization depends on the successful completion of the following functions:

1. *Formulation of a code.* An individual, or a group of individuals, constructs a new, utopian image of socio-cultural organization. This model is a blueprint of an ideal society or "goal culture." Contrasted with the goal culture is the existing culture, which is presented as inadequate or evil in certain respects. Connecting the existing culture and the goal culture is a transfer culture: a system of operations which, if faithfully carried out, will transform the existing culture into the goal culture. Failure to institute the transfer operations will, according to the code, result in either the perpetuation of the existing misery or the ultimate destruction of the society (if not of the whole world). Not infrequently the code, or the core of it, is formulated by one individual in the course of a hallucinatory revelation; such prophetic experiences are apt to launch religiously oriented movements, since the source of the revelation is apt to be regarded as a supernatural being. Non-hallucinatory formulations usually are found in politically oriented movements. In either case, the formulation of the code constitutes a reformulation of the author's own mazeway, and

often brings to him a renewed confidence in the future and a remission of the complaints he experienced before.

2. *Communication.* The formulators of the code preach the code to other people in an evangelistic spirit. The aim of the communication is to make converts. The code is offered as the means of spiritual salvation for the individual and of cultural salvation for the society. Promises of benefit to the target population need not be immediate or materialistic, for the basis of the code's appeal is the attractiveness of identification with a more highly organized system, with all that this implies in the way of self-respect. Indeed, in view of the extensiveness of the changes in values often implicit in such codes, appeal to currently held values would often be pointless. Religious codes offer spiritual salvation, identification with God, elect status; political codes offer honor, fame, the respect of society for sacrifices made in its interest. But refusal to accept the code is usually defined as placing the listener in immediate spiritual, as well as material, peril with respect to his existing values. In small societies, the target population may be the entire community; but in more complex societies, the message may be aimed only at certain groups deemed eligible for participation in the transfer and goal cultures.

3. *Organization.* The code attracts converts. The motivations which are satisfied by conversion, and the psychodynamics of the conversion experience itself, are likely to be highly diverse, ranging from the mazeway resynthesis characteristic of the prophet, and the hysterical conviction of the "true believer," to the calculating expediency of the opportunist. As the group of converts expands, it differentiates into two parts: a set of disciples and a set of mass followers. The disciples increasingly become the executive organization, responsible for administering the evangelistic program, pro-

tecting the formulator, combatting heresy, and so on. In this role, the disciples increasingly become full-time specialists in the work of the movement. In this they are economically supported by the mass followers who continue to play their roles in the existing culture, devoting part of their time and money to the movement. The tricornered relationship between the formulators, the disciples, and the mass followers is given an authoritarian structure, even without the formalities of older organizations, by the charismatic quality of the formulator's image. The formulator is regarded as a man to whom, from a supernatural being or from some other source of wisdom unavailable to the mass, a superior knowledge and authority has been vouchsafed which justifies his claim to unquestioned belief and obedience from his followers.

4. *Adaptation.* Because the movement is a revolutionary organization (however benevolent and humane the ultimate values to which it subscribes), it threatens the interests of any group which obtains advantage, or believes it obtains advantage, from maintaining or only moderately reforming the status quo. Furthermore, the code is never complete; new inadequacies are constantly being found in the existing culture, and new inconsistencies, predictive failures, and ambiguities discovered in the code itself (some of the latter being pointed out by the opposition). The response of the code formulators and disciples is to rework the code, and, if necessary, to defend the movement by political and diplomatic maneuver, and, ultimately, by force. The general tendency is for codes to harden gradually, and for the tone of the movement to become increasingly nativistic and hostile both toward non-participating fellow-members of society, who will

ultimately be defined as "traitors," and toward "national enemies."

5. *Cultural transformation.* If the movement is able to capture both the adherence of a substantial proportion of a local population and, in complex societies, of the functionally crucial apparatus (such as power and communications networks, water supply, transport systems, and military establishment), the transfer culture and, in some cases, the goal culture itself, can be put into operation. The revitalization, if successful, will be attended by the drastic decline of the quasi-pathological individual symptoms of anomie and by the disappearance of the cultural distortions. For such a revitalization to be accomplished, however, the movement must be able to maintain its boundaries from outside invasion, must be able to obtain internal social conformity without destructive coercion, and must have a successful economic system.

6. *Routinization.* If the preceding functions are satisfactorily completed, the functional reasons for the movement's existence as an innovative force disappear. The transfer culture, if not the goal culture, is operating, of necessity with the participation of a large proportion of the community. Although the movement's leaders may resist the realization of the fact, the movement's function shifts from the role of innovation to the role of maintenance. If the movement was heavily religious in orientation, its legacy is a cult or church which preserves and reworks the code, and maintains, through ritual and myth, the public awareness of the history and values which brought forth the new culture. If the movement was primarily political, its organization is routinized into various stable decision-making, and morale-and-order-maintaining functions (such as ad-

ministrative offices, police, and military bodies). Charisma can, to a degree, be routinized, but its intensity diminishes as its functional necessity becomes, with increasing obviousness, outmoded.

V. THE NEW STEADY STATE   With the routinization of the movement, a new steady state may be said to exist. Steady-state processes of culture change continue; many of them are in areas where the movement has made further change likely. In particular, changes in the value structure of the culture may lay the basis for long-continuing changes (such as the train of economic and technological consequences of the dissemination of the Protestant ethic after the Protestant Reformation). Thus, in addition to the changes which the movement accomplishes during its active phase, it may control the direction of the subsequent equilibrium processes by shifting the values which define the cultural focus. The record of the movement itself, over time, gradually is subject to distortion, and eventually is enshrined in myths and rituals which elevate the events which occurred, and persons who acted, into quasi- or literally divine status.

Two psychological mechanisms seem to be of peculiar importance in the revitalization process: mazeway resynthesis (Wallace, 1956a, 1956b), and hysterical conversion. The resynthesis is most dramatically exemplified in the career of the prophet who formulates a new religious code during a hallucinatory trance. Typically, such persons, after suffering increasing depreciation of self-esteem as the result of their inadequacy to achieve the culturally ideal standards, reach a point of either physical or drug-induced exhaustion, during which a resynthesis of values and beliefs occurs. The resynthesis is, like other innovations, a recombination of pre-existing configurations; the uniqueness of this particular process is the suddenness of conviction, the trancelike state of the subject, and the emotionally central nature of the subject matter. There is some reason to suspect that such dramatic resyntheses depend on a special biochemical milieu, accompanying the "stage of exhaustion" of the stress (in Selye's sense) syndrome, or on a similar milieu induced by drugs. But comparable resyntheses are, of course, sometimes accomplished more slowly, without the catalytic aid of extreme stress or drugs. This kind of resynthesis produces, apparently, a permanent alteration of mazeway: the new stable cognitive configuration, is, as it were, constructed out of the materials of earlier configurations which, once rearranged, cannot readily reassemble into the older forms.

The hysterical conversion is more typical of the mass follower who is repeatedly subjected to suggestion by a charismatic leader and an excited crowd. The convert of this type may, during conversion, display various dissociative behaviors (rage, speaking in tongues, rolling on the ground, weeping, etc.). After conversion, his overt behavior may be in complete conformity with the code to which he has been exposed. But his behavior has changed, not because of a radical resynthesis, but because of the adoption under suggestion of an additional social personality which temporarily replaces, but does not destroy, the earlier. He remains, in a sense, a case of multiple personality and is liable, if removed from reinforcing symbols, to lapse into an earlier social personality. The participant in the lynch mob or in the camp meeting revival is a familiar example of this type of convert. But persons can be maintained in this state of hysterical conversion for months or years, if the "trance" is continuously maintained by the symbolic

environment (flags, statues, portraits, songs, etc.) and
continuous suggestion (speeches, rallies, etc.). The
most familiar contemporary example is the German
under Hitler who participated in the Nazi genocide
program, but reverted to *Gemütlichkeit* when the war
ended. The difference between the resynthesized person
and the converted one does not lie in the nature of the
codes to which they subscribe (they may be the same),
but in the blandness and readiness of the hysterical convert to revert, as compared to the almost paranoid intensity and stability of the resynthesized prophet. A
successful movement, by virtue of its ability to maintain
suggestion continuously for years, is able to hold the
hysterical convert indefinitely, or even to work a real
resynthesis by repeatedly forcing him, after hysterical
conversion, to re-examine his older values and beliefs
and to work through to a valid resynthesis, sometimes
under considerable stress. The Chinese Communists, for
instance, apparently have become disillusioned by hysterical conversions and have used various techniques,
some coercive and some not, but all commonly lumped
together as "brain-washing" in Western literature, to
induce valid resynthesis. The aim of these communist
techniques, like those of the established religions, is,
literally, to produce a "new man."

It is impossible to exaggerate the importance of these
two psychological processes for culture change, for they
make possible the rapid substitution of a new cultural
Gestalt for an old, and thus the rapid cultural transformation of whole populations. Without this mechanism,
the cultural transformation of the 600,000,000 people
of China by the Communists could not have occurred;
nor the Communist-led revitalization and expansion of
the USSR; nor the American Revolution; nor the Protestant Reformation; nor the rise and spread of Christi-

anity, Mohammedanism, and Buddhism. In the written historical record, revitalization movements begin with Ikhnaton's ultimately disastrous attempt to establish a new, monotheistic religion in Egypt; they are found, continent by continent, in the history of all human societies, occurring with frequency proportional to the pressures to which the society is subjected. For small tribal societies, in chronically extreme situations, movements may develop every ten or fifteen years; in stable complex cultures, the rate of a society-wide movement may be one every two or three hundred years.

In view of the frequency and geographical diversity of revitalization movements, it can be expected that their content will be extremely varied, corresponding to the diversity of situational contexts and cultural backgrounds in which they develop. Major culture areas are, over extended periods of time, associated with particular types: New Guinea and Melanesia, during the latter part of the nineteenth and the twentieth centuries, has been the home of the well-known "cargo cults." The most prominent feature of these cults is the expectation that the ancestors soon will arrive in a steamship, bearing a cargo of the white man's goods, and will lead a nativistic revolution culminating in the ejection of European masters. The Indians of the eastern half of South America for centuries after the conquest set off on migrations for the *terre sans mal* where a utopian way of life, free of Spaniards and Portuguese, would be found; North American Indians of the eighteenth and nineteenth centuries were prone to revivalistic movements such as the Ghost Dance, whose adherents believed that appropriate ritual and the abandonment of the sins of the white man would bring a return of the golden age before contact; South Africa has been the home of the hundreds of small, enthusiastic, separatist churches which have broken free of the missionary organizations. As might be expected, a congruence evidently exists between the cultural *Anlage* and the content of movement which, together with processes of direct and stimulus diffusion, accounts for the tendency for movements to fall into areal types.

CULTURAL ABANDONMENT, CULTURAL STABILITY, AND THE REACTION TO CULTURAL LOSS

IN THE EARLIER DISCUSSIONS of innovation, we did not explicitly deal with the process of cultural abandonment. While much of innovation is cumulative, in the sense that new configurations are added to an existing stock, there is usually a correlative process of deletion: as new content is added, old content is abandoned. Where express dissatisfaction with the old configuration is the motive for innovation, the two processes are often so closely associated that the relationship is not seen as problematical. Thus, for instance, in urban areas the introduction of the electric light is associated with the abandonment of oil lamps. But from time to time, the anthropologist is confronted with cases of the abandonment by a society of culture traits, or even major *Gestalten,* without the acceptance of any visibly superior substitute. He is also confronted with many circumstances in which his ingenuity in functional analysis is stretched to its limits—sometimes, beyond these limits—to account for the refusal of people to abandon components of their cultural system which, from one theoretical viewpoint or another, ought to have been abandoned. Cultures appear to possess a stability which is difficult to account for by simple psychological principles, such as the law of effect. Finally, since the development of serious interest in the psychology of acculturation, the anthropologist has been interested in the apparently psychopathological responses of people to unplanned and unintended cultural loss. Indeed, as we remarked in the previous chapter, a part of culture-and-personality theory has been explicitly concerned with the damaging "impact" of culture change on personality structure.

The classic cases of cultural abandonment would seem to be those inexplicable periods of decline which seem to afflict great civilizations, such as the Roman Empire, Greece, and imperial Spain. It is difficult to account for such phenomena by functional arguments without postulating a lesion of some component, whose failure sets in motion a train of functionally inevitable disasters which result in the ultimate collapse of the system. But where to find the lesion? Here, speculative historians have a free field to adduce anything, from a decline in hay production to the equality of women to genetic inbreeding, as the source of the lesion. Such particularistic speculations, however, are often no more convincing than metaphysical appeals to the law of entropy or the theory of cycles. Nor, in such cases, is it always possible to find some overwhelming external interference of the kind which we have suggested, as the precipitants of a pre-revitalization slump in organization. One is left, in fact, with the suspicion (already voiced in the discussion of the "genius" of cultures) that not all functioning socio-cultural systems are in stable equilibrium, but rather that some—and these are the ones we are now discussing—are in a state of gradually increasing oscillation, or are following an exponential curve in regard to some crucial parameter; their demise is the inevitable consequence of the uninterrupted operation of their own internal laws. This consideration leads us to suspect that not merely whole civilizations, but also—and perhaps more typically—particular institutions and customs are governed by processual laws which make their obsolescence and abandonment inevitable. Still other sub-systems, particularly economic ones, may be governed by processual principles which make their operation cyclical; for example, the trading stamp industry in the United States which, within any one state, is characterized by a cycle from legalization, through partial acceptance, to universal acceptance (at which point it becomes merely an expense without advantage to any storekeeper), to prohibition, to legalization again.

But from the psychological standpoint, the critical issue is the determination of the point in the process of increasing disfunction at which the group jettisons the disfunctional cultural equipment. In a general way, it may be suggested that the jettison point will lie somewhere *beyond* the point at which the average individual member of the group recognizes that maintenance of the institution will cost him more than any alternative in the near future. The actual jettisoning will probably occur, beyond this point, after respected community agencies publicly propose abandonment. An example of the process in the anthropological literature is given by the abandonment of taboos in Hawaii, by the forsaking of burdensome religious rituals among Mayan descendants in Guatemala, and by the relinquishment of torture among the eighteenth-century Iroquois. The emotional cost of cultural abandonment, however, even in the presence of an immediately recognizable functional substitute, is remarkably high. It is suspected that it is this high psychological cost of abandonment itself, rather than continued reinforcement, which is responsible for some of the remarkable phenomena of cultural stability.

Let us therefore examine the nature of these costs of abandonment.

The most dramatic demonstration of the psychological need to maintain the image of cultural continuity is provided by behavioral responses to the impact of disasters. Immediately following a sudden, unexpected impact (such as a tornado or atomic explosion) which wreaks extensive physical damage and kills or injures many people, many survivors, both injured and uninjured, experience what has been called the "disaster syndrome." This is a behavior sequence which may last for minutes, hours, or days, depending on individual circumstances. In the first stage, the individual is described as being "dazed," "stunned," "apathetic," "passive," "aimless." He is (literally) apt to be insensitive to pain, to be almost completely unaware, consciously, of his own injuries or of the seriousness of the injuries of others, and to ignore the extent of the visible damage. Thus, first-stage victims will do trivial things, such as sweeping off the doorstep of a flattened house, or will leave seriously injured kinfolk in order to chat with neighbors. In the second stage, the individual is no longer dazed, but he becomes pathetically eager for support and reassurance that known persons, structures, and institutions have survived. Personal loss is minimized; concern is for reassurance that the community is intact. Persons in this stage can be easily led and formed into work teams, but they are not effective in leadership. In the third stage, a mildly euphoric altruism obtains: the individual enthusiastically participates in group activity, designed to restore and rehabilitate the community. Observers remark on the high morale and selfless dedication to be seen on all sides. Finally, as the euphoria wears off, there is full awareness of the long-term effects of personal and community loss. Complaint and criticism against public agencies, bickering with neighbors, and dismay over the personal cost of the disaster attain full consciousness. This syndrome has been repeatedly identified in the aftermath of both natural and wartime disasters (Wallace, 1956d; Wolfenstein, 1957) and in the responses of target groups in cultural crises (Reina, 1958).

The theoretical importance of the disaster syndrome lies in the fact that large physical disasters present an almost laboratory-pure situation of cultural loss. Individuals, one moment secure in their status as members of an ongoing community with an effective culture, next are shorn of much of the tangible evidence of that culture. An initial fantasy, reported by some survivors of the Worcester tornado, was that this was the end of the world. Such an impression should not appear bizarre to an anthropologist, for, in a sense, this impression is valid: even though the physical destruction is not complete, the damage in casualties, and in material loss, inevitably must shatter the existing *Gestalt* by virtue of the principle of functional interdependence.

The deprivation of data which confirm to the individual his psychological set, his "mazeway," arouses shattering anxiety and is followed by denial: the individual virtually blots out awareness of injury and loss. Related phenomena would seem to be the "denial" of anxiety-provoking sensory isolation by means of hallucination in the well-known psychological experiments; the sequences of disturbance and denial, elicited by perceptual disconfirmation—"cognitive dissonance"—as analyzed by psychologists (Festinger, 1957); the refusal to admit death in the mourning process; and, in general, neurotic fears of abandoning a non-gratifying response. The psychological principle behind all these manifestations is fundamental to any theory of cultural stability and culture change; it may be expressed as a Principle of Conservation of Cognitive Structure: (1) the individual will not abandon *any* particular conception of reality (including, therefore, his culturally standard conceptions), even in the face of direct evidence of its current inutility, without having had an opportunity to construct a new mazeway, with or without substitute conceptions, in which the invalid conception is not a functionally necessary component; (2) initial confrontation of the individual with evidence of inutility will arouse an anxiety-denial syndrome, and this anxiety-denial response may continue for a considerable period of time; (3) it is easier for the individual to abandon a conception if substitutes are offered and models of new mazeways are presented, than if the abandonment must be made "blind," in response to awareness of the inutility of the concept (cf. Wallace, 1957; Conant, 1951). A corollary of this principle is the "dilemma of immobility": individuals for years will cling to a disordered socio-cultural system, in which events do not follow reliably upon their supposed antecedents, rather than face the anxiety of cultural abandonment.

This dilemma is particularly poignant in acculturation situations where an acceptable alternative cultural system exists, which the group would willingly accept, even at the cost of giving up shreds of the older culture, but which cannot be adopted because of active interference by a "prejudiced" and discriminatory and dominant society. Often, in such situations, insult is added to injury by the dominant group expressing severe contempt for the disorderly nature of the subordinate group, even while it may prevent the exchange for something better. The emotional dilemma of the individual, who is entrapped in such a situation, is productive of severe anxiety and, secondarily, of quasi-pathological defenses. He is caught, on the one hand, between shame at, and lack of confidence in, his "own" truncated disorderly system, and, on the other, fear that if he abandons parts of this admittedly inadequate culture, he will merely restrict himself to an existence which is no more orderly than before and is considerably smaller. Evidence of the personality damage resulting from chronically corrosive situations of this type is one of the standard features of the culture-and-personality literature. Hallowell's data on the Ojibwa personality under (retarded) acculturation, are perhaps the best known. In a series of papers comparing the relatively unacculturated Ojibwa of the Lake Winnipeg region with the more acculturated people of northern Wisconsin (Hallowell, 1955), he found, in both Rorschach records and general behavioral data, evidence that the partly acculturated Ojibwa personality was a "regressive" (i.e., quasi-pathological) version of the unacculturated personality. In view of the economic uncertainty of Wisconsin Ojibwa life, the relatively low social status, and the presence of the standard dilemma of immobility—unreliability of existing culture, unavailability of an acceptable substitute—this evidence of personality damage is not unexpected. Similar findings were reported by Kardiner and Ovesey (1951) on the American Negro, for whom the problems of cultural and ethnic identification assume major significance, even in individual psychodynamics. The "marginal man," indeed, is an ideal type constructed to label persons caught precisely in the vortex of such dilemmas, unable to forsake the old culture, yet, because of experience in the new, unable to be happy in it either.

The resolution of such "dilemmas of immobility" can, it would seem, normally come about via any combination of three processes: (1) revitalization; (2) assimilation; (3) nativism or nationalism. We have already discussed revitalization at some length as a deliberate syncretic cultural reorganization within a definably bounded social group. Assimilation and nativism (or nationalism), without revitalization (although revitalization movements may be nativistic or nationalistic) are most apt to occur in the subordinate society in an acculturation situation. In assimilation, the subordinate group attempts to abandon its existing inadequate culture by entering into the society of the dominant group and accepting its culture, almost *in toto* (retaining only token vestiges of their distinctive culture traits). This is the course adopted by many American Negroes, especially in recent years, in the United States. Pure nativism or nationalism, with no effort at revitalization (Ames, 1957), is often military in character and is motivated by a desire to rid the group of the presence of members of the dominant group who are the source of constant shame-producing reminders of cultural inferiority, as well as of practical interference. An example of this is the so-called Black Hawk War, in Illinois and Wisconsin, in 1832. A band of displaced and humiliated Sac, Fox, and Kickapoo, under the warrior Black Hawk, attempted to retain their settlements on ceded land, east of the Mississippi, in the face of eviction orders. Their actions were interpreted by the United States as a military attack and the group of about one thousand men, women, and children virtually was exterminated. But much nativism and nationalism is not military in character; it takes the form of stubborn ideological denial of cultural inadequacy, with withdrawal and deliberate insularity as, for instance, in religious groups such as the Amish and Hutterites.

[V]

Culture and
Mental Illness

Wᴇ ꜱʜᴀʟʟ ɴᴏᴡ ᴄᴏɴꜱɪᴅᴇʀ the relationship between the culture of a society and the forms and frequencies of the mental diseases suffered by the members of that society.

It is necessary to begin this chapter with a caution. The anthropological student of mental illness must beware of gross semantic chasms which lie hidden beneath the seemingly objective and scientific surface of psychiatry, clinical psychology, and affiliated fields, including his own. Even the relationship between the meanings of the terms "mental health" and "mental disease" is a trap for the unwary, for, as Jahoda (1958) points out, for many writers "mental health" does not mean merely an absence of "mental disease," nor "mental disease" merely the reciprocal absence of "mental health." Many persons belong in a vaguely bounded middle category, characterized neither by positive mental health nor by definite mental illness. It is the questionable size and composition of this middle category that produces part of the semantic difficulty, for each authority sets the boundaries at different points on the scale.

For the anthropologist, who must consider mental health and mental illness in exotic non-Western cultures and in cross-cultural comparison, the semantic ambiguities of Western science are compounded by the diversity with which human cultures conceive of, and respond to, illness, and by the variety of the forms of illness themselves. "Hysteria," "possession," and "schizoid," for instance, are terms used by anthropologists in contexts where their significance, as labels for psychiatric disorder, is questionable, to say the least. Despite equivalence of process, that which is regarded as "illness" in one society may be regarded as merely one aspect of the normal and healthy life in another. The anthropologist's well-intentioned effort, both to apply the concepts of Western science as descriptive categories and to reflect the psychological reality of the native world, thus frequently entangles him in semantic conflicts.

Efforts to resolve these conflicts have inspired a small body of anthropological literature, devoted to the elaboration of cross-culturally valid definitions of mental illnesses and of the concept of mental illness itself (*vide* Benedict and Jacks, 1954; Devereux, 1956; Wegrocki, 1939; Opler, 1956; Linton, 1956). Treatment and hospitalization are obviously invalid criteria, because only a few societies in the ethnographer's universe have institutionalized the Western psychiatric concepts and have mental hospitals. The anthropological definitions, therefore, generally center about some notion of behavioral deviance or abnormality as the universal sign of mental illness. Such a definition may refer to statistical distribution as the locus of the abnormal, or it may emphasize non-conformity with appropriate behavioral pattern, rather than rarity, as the criterion of abnormality. The advantage of such a definition lies in the fact that it does not beg questions of symptomatology, etiology, or prognosis, and in effect utilizes the social diagnosis of the society itself as the measure of behavioral normality. The disadvantage of such a definition is that it tends to ignore (or to cover only by speculation) the phenomenology of the individual's private motives, beliefs, and feelings of anxiety, sorrow, conflict, and so forth.

TYPES OF MENTAL ILLNESS

DESPITE THE AFOREMENTIONED uncertainty as to the proper abstract definition of mental illness, and despite the eloquent pleas of "dynamic" psychiatrists to abjure the "static" categories of mere "descriptive" psychiatry, it is of fundamental importance to describe and name classes of psychopathological phenomena, according to some rational schema, in order to plan treatment and to define an orderly research program. European and American psychiatrists have, in clinical practice during the past half century, developed a working descriptive typology of mental diseases which is serviceable, if not logically elegant. The grosser categories of this typology, after a few culturally-specific allusions are pruned away, are usable by the anthropologist for cross-cultural purposes. The schema which follows is based on the *Diagnostic and Statistical Manual: Mental Disorders* of the American Psychiatric Association, which was published in 1952 after a careful analysis of clinical and research practice. Because of the importance of identifying the range of the phenomena with which the anthropologist interested in culture and mental illness must deal, we shall present the over-all typology in some detail.

Two main categories of mental disease are recognized in the *Manual:* (1) "Disorders Caused By or Associated

With Impairment of Brain Tissue Function"; (2) "Disorders of Psychogenic Origin or Without Clearly Defined Physical Cause or Structural Change in the Brain." The respective symptomatologies overlap almost completely: hallucinations, delusions, disorientation, impoverishment of memory, and a long list of other behavioral disturbances occur in both the organic and the functional categories. Indeed, it may be difficult to assign a given case confidently to one category or the other, without extensive laboratory and psychological testing. The differentiation essentially is based on the principle that, where an organic disturbance of brain tissue is *known* to be the precipitating factor, the disease is classified as a disorder of brain function; where no such organic disturbance is *known* to be responsible, the illness is classified as "psychogenic" or "functional," etc. A given case may be classified under both categories (for instance, a mental defective who is also psychotic).

All of the organic brain disorders are characterized by a basic common syndrome, consisting of:

1. Impairment of orientation in time and space
2. Impairment of memory
3. Impairment of all intellectual functions (comprehension, calculation, knowledge, learning, etc.)
4. Impairment of judgment
5. Instability and shallowness of affect

Frequently, hallucinations, delusions, and various behavior disturbances are displayed by the organic disorder. They are divided further into three main groups: (1) acute brain disorders, which are reversible; (2) chronic brain disorders, which are not reversible, and (3) mental deficiency.

The acute brain syndromes are produced by intracranial infections (encephalitis, meningitis, abscess, etc.); by systemic infection (pneumonia, typhoid fever, acute rheumatic fever); by drug or poison intoxication (barbiturates, opiates, hormones, lead, gases, etc.); by alcoholic intoxication (acute drunkenness and delirium tremens); by severe physical injury (accident, gunshot, surgery); by circulatory disturbance (cerebral embolism, arterial hypertension, etc.); by convulsive disorder ("idiopathic" epilepsy); by metabolic disturbance (as in uremia, diabetes, hyperthyroidism, vitamin deficiency, etc.); by intra-cranial neoplasm (tumors), and by various diseases of unknown or uncertain cause (such as multiple sclerosis).

The chronic brain syndromes may be the product of congenital cranial anomaly, producing some degree of mental deficiency (as in congenital spastic paraplegia, Mongolism, prenatal maternal infectious disease, birth trauma, etc.); of syphilis of central nervous system; of cerebral arteriosclerosis; of senile brain disease; of various disturbances of metabolism, growth, or nutrition (pellagra and other vitamin deficiency diseases, various endocrine disorders, etc.); of diseases of unknown cause (multiple sclerosis, Pick's disease, Huntington's chorea), and of any of the determinants of the acute brain disorders, if the disorder is later found to be chronic.

The third, separate, category is mental deficiency. Here are classified "those cases presenting primarily a defect of intelligence existing since birth, without demonstrated organic brain disease or known prenatal cause."

The remainder of the known mental disorders thus are placed in a residual category of non-congenital disorders in which no known physical impairment of brain tissue function has been demonstrated as yet and in which, in some instances, the origin may be "psychogenic." Most of the theoretical and research activity of social scientists has been devoted to this large residual category, with the conspicuous exception of mental deficiency (Sarason and Gladwin, 1958). This residual category is divided into five sub-categories: psychosis; psychosomatic disorder; neurosis; personality disorder; and transient situational personality disorder.

The psychoses in general are characterized by personality disintegration, impairment of intellectual functions, and social failure. This characterization, of course, is very close to the characterization of the brain syndromes, and the differential diagnosis is based on the absence of evidence of brain tissue disfunction more than on clearcut behavioral distinctions. As before, hallucinations, delusions, and disorganized overt behavior may be present. The psychoses are further divided into four major categories: the involutional psychotic reaction (depressions, primarily in women, during menopause); affective reactions (oscillating manic-depressive reactions and relatively stable depressive reactions); pure paranoid reactions (which are extremely rare); and schizophrenic reactions (formerly denoted by the term "dementia praecox").

The "psychosomatic category" is labeled "Psychophysiologic Autonomic and Visceral Disorders" in order to exclude the conversion hysterias, and because the expression "psychosomatic" alone has come to denote a point of view toward the medical sciences as a whole, rather than a specific group of diseases. Such disorders include a wide panorama: skin diseases, anorexia, loss of weight, menstrual and endocrine disturbances, hypertension, cramps, neurasthenic fatigue, certain asthmatic conditions, and so forth.

The psychoneurotic disorders, characterized by chronic anxiety and periodic or constant "maladjustment," but lacking the gross personality, intellectual, and social impairments of the psychoses are classified under six headings: anxiety reaction (formerly called "anxiety state"); dissociative reaction (such as depersonalization, dissociated personality, stupor, fugue, amnesia, dream state, somnambulism, etc.); conversion reaction (such as anesthesia, paralysis, tremor, tic, etc.); phobic reaction (fear of syphilis, dirt, closed places, high places, open places, animals, etc.); obsessive compulsive reaction (touching, counting, ceremonials, handwashing, or recurring thoughts, etc.); and depressive reaction (of less malignant severity than in the psychoses).

The remainder are classified as personality disorders and transient situational personality disorders. These include such categories as "inadequate" personality, schizoid personality, cyclothymic personality, paranoid personality, emotionally unstable personality, passive-aggressive personality, and compulsive personality. The category "sociopathic personality disturbance," which covers alcoholic and drug addiction, sexual deviation, habitual criminality, and the so-called "psychopathic personality" ("chronically antisocial individuals"), is also included. The "transient" disorders include "gross stress reactions" (reversible psychopathology, of almost any symptomatic variety, precipitated by severe physical or emotional stress, such as combat or disaster) and equally various "adjustment reactions," temporarily mimicking all sorts of more serious chronic disturbances, characteristic of various age groups (e.g., "low morale" in adults, sleeping difficulties in infants, truancy in children, etc.). In our view, this melange of disapproved behaviors, together with outright criminality, are "diseases" only to the extent that all behavior, including that which is socially undesirable, is determined by forces beyond the control of the individual. Hence, in this chapter, we shall not devote our attention to such categories as alcoholism, suicide, crime, and drug addiction, which may or may not be culturally defined as delinquencies and may or may not be symptoms of diseases which fall under other categories, such as schizophrenia. Their relevance to theories of mental illness is a subject which goes beyond the scope of this chapter.

THEORIES OF THE "CAUSES" OF MENTAL ILLNESS

THE DISCERNING READER will already have recognized some of the implications of a point made in the preceding section: that the disorders involving physical impairment of brain tissue are distinguished not by their symptomatology, but by the fact that an organic deficiency is known to be the (or a) cause (in the sense of a preceding complex of circumstances sufficient to bring about the onset of the disorder). In a broad sense, then, "theory" is not necessary to account for these disorders; *the* cause, in most instances, is known, and the *kind* of cause is assumed to be physical in all instances. The research and clinical problem is simply to identify the specific physical lesion or deficiency responsible for a given disorder.

The remainder (which constitute the second category) of the mental disorders are the subject of endless theorizing, considerable research, and not very much positive knowledge, either with regard to etiology or treatment. The aim of scientific research must be to determine the necessary and sufficient conditions under which a class of phenomena occur. But neuro-psychiatric science is far from being able to state these conditions for *any* of the "functional" (i.e., not definitely known to be organic) mental disorders. Two major schools of thought at present contend (with minimal mutual lip service) with respect to etiological and therapeutic theories: the biochemical and the psycho-social. The biochemical school primarily orients itself to the psychoses and concerns itself with identifying those currently unknown anomalies of body chemistry (in blood, endocrine secretions, neural tissue, etc.) which are responsible for psychosis, and with discovering the appropriate physical therapies for correcting such anomalies (cf. Kety, 1959; Kallman, 1938). Thus, the biochemical school, in effect, expects to bring the psychoses over into the category of organically-determined mental disorders. The psycho-social school embraces the various psycho-analytic disciplines, social and clinical psychology, and (for the most part) sociology and anthropology. While this school is heterogeneous, it shares a common faith that it is in some distortion of the subject's social learning experience and current social situation that his psychopathology originates. Theories vary, however, with respect to the locus of the responsible distortion: psychoanalytic and social anthropological theories tend to emphasize early experience, particularly the parents' relationship to the child; sociologic theories tend to emphasize ecological and social class factors, and so on. With respect to cultural anthropology's participation in the scientific investigation of mental illness, the most glaring weakness has been the bland assumption that "mental disorder" (a few outstanding organic complaints apart) is caused by disorders in social, cultural, and psychological processes This bland assumption in part has been based on failure to consider seriously the fact that the various known organic impairments can and do regularly produce symptomatologies practically indistinguishable from the whole gamut of "functional" symptomatologies, ranging from psychosis to the transient situational reactions. It has also in part been based on neglect of the existing evidence for genetic and biochemical complicity in the development of the supposedly "psychogenic" or "functional" psychoses. Since cultural anthropologists generally are consulted by, and read the works of, those psychiatrists and psychologists who are committed to the psycho-social tradition, this bias is not corrected from outside the field, but remains to stunt the development of cultural anthropological research in this important area.

In view of its importance for the theoretical orientation of students of anthropology, a brief outline is here given of a theory which attempts to relate biochemical and psycho-social processes in mental disease. Of all the psychoses, the schizophrenic syndrome is probably the most common. It is the writer's opinion that this psychosis is precipitated and maintained by a biochemical disorder or disorders for which hereditary predisposition is common. Biochemical deficiency reduces the "semantic capacity" of the individual below the level necessary for adequate cultural participation. From the microcosmic viewpoint, this critical level is the boundary between normalcy and deviancy; from the organization viewpoint, it is the degree of diversity which the individual must be able to maintain in a state of relative orderliness, acceptable to self and others. Such a semantic decrement is experienced by the victim as a condition of relative meaninglessness or, as the psychiatrist puts it, as "feelings of unreality" and "lack of affect." These experiences of desemantication may, or may not, be accompanied by other disturbing phenomena, such as hallucination and hypochondriacal sensations. From the initial desemantication flows, inevitably, a set of consequences: a deterioration of the victim's existing personality structure; the development of increasingly desperate and generally inadequate "psychotic" defenses, intended to forestall social extrusion;

and, eventually, social extrusion in some form or other. This theory recognizes that cultural differences will be reflected in the symptomatic content and the prevalence of the syndrome in various populations, but relies upon the concept of the cultural capacity of the individual to relate biochemical and psycho-social processes in the individual case (cf. Wallace, 1960b).

CURRENT CONCEPTIONS OF THE RELATIONS OF CULTURE AND MENTAL ILLNESS

CURRENT CONCEPTIONS of the relationship of culture to mental illness may be conveniently classified under four headings: cultural epidemiology; culture as providing the pathogenic process; culture as providing the therapeutic process; and culture itself, as affected by mental disorder.

CULTURAL EPIDEMIOLOGY

THE EPIDEMIOLOGY OF MENTAL DISEASE considers the distribution of mental disorders of various kinds over a number of variables, only one of which is culture; others are sex, age, migration history, social class, education, morbidity in other disease categories, nutritional level, ecological zone, and so on. Most of these other categories are, however, not independent of culture and, consequently, are definitely relevant to culturally-oriented inquiries.

From the days of the earliest systematic ethnological fieldwork, up to the present time, anthropologists have been interested in the fact that the symptoms of mental disorder vary, depending on the cultural context of the victim. Sometimes the patterning of these symptoms is so unlike Western clinical portraits as to suggest that a new mental disease has been discovered. Familiar examples may be cited: amok and latah in Southeast Asia; piblokto among Eskimo, and arctic hysteria among northern Siberian peoples; the windigo psychosis among northeastern Algonkian forest hunters. Even within Western society, as Opler has demonstrated, the nature of the symptoms typically exhibited by members of such ethnic groups as Irish and Italians, in New York City, is sharply different: Irish male schizophrenics tend to be quiet and withdrawn, and their Italian counterparts tend to be noisy and aggressive (Opler and Singer, 1956). These differences do not, however, justify the imputation of a different disease category. Windigo psychosis, with its common pattern of somatic delusions, ideas of reference, supernatural persecution complex, and "cannibalistic panic," is a precise image of paranoid schizophrenia, as observed in Western man, except that the overt ideas of persecution or influence of Western man are apt to be oriented toward different supernatural beings or even toward other humans (such as "the men in the Kremlin" or "the FBI"), and to emphasize sex rather than food (the cannibalistic panic being replaced by the homosexual panic). Most such "ethnic psychoses," which reflect in their behavior the specific cultural content of the victim's society, are simply local varieties of a common disease process to which human beings, as such, are vulnerable. In this light, then, all mental disorders must be considered to reflect, in symptomatic content, the victim's past and present cultural environment.

CULTURE AS PATHOGENIC INFLUENCE

IF WE CONCLUDE that the major categories of mental disorder are universal types of human affliction, even though cultural differences are responsible for conspicuous local differences in the content of symptomatology, we must still ask whether cultural differences are associated with differences in the frequency of illness in the major, and universal, diagnostic classifications. Despite semantic difficulties, and notwithstanding the scattered nature of the material, two general conclusions concerning cultural epidemiology can be made: (1) culturally differentiated populations do vary measurably in the incidence (the number of persons who contract a disease during a specified period of time, usually taken as a year) of one or another of the various disease entities, a fact which suggests that, whatever the etiological factors are, in part they are culturally determined; and (2), culturally differentiated populations do vary measurably in the prevalence (the number of persons who suffer from a disease during a specified period of time) of one or another of the various disease categories. These generalizations suggest strongly that, whatever the therapeutic and chronicity factors are, their incidence and prevalence in part are culturally determined.

Epidemiological inquiries essentially are based on demographic and social survey statistics. Clinical observation, however, is the source of the data and intuitions which point to the role of culture as a pathogenic influence. Such a putative influence is considered to be direct when the very structure of human relations, and the beliefs and values commonly held in a society, are conceived to be necessarily productive of psychological conflict and anxiety in individuals who participate in the organization. The influence may be considered as indirect when the mere participation in the socio-cultural organization is not, in itself, considered sufficient to elicit psychopathology.

Culture as Indirect Pathogenic Influence

LET US CONSIDER the indirect pathogenic influence first. A particularly clear example of such an influence is given by studies of the mental disorders accompanying *trypanosomiasis* ("sleeping sickness"), a general infection transmitted to man by the bite of the infected tsetse fly. This disorder is said to be "the commonest cause of mental derangement throughout large areas of West Africa" (Tooth, 1950), and is difficult, if not impossible, to distinguish from schizophrenia without identification of the trypanosome micro-organism in the body fluids. The symptomatic picture in "tryps" is as variable as that in "true" schizophrenia, and the same types of behavioral disorder may be found in either. But, in line with the distinction described earlier, one (tryps) is an "organic" psychosis and the other (schizophrenia) is not.

The type of tryps to which most psychiatric attention has been paid is that carried by the flies *Glossina palpalis* and *Glossina tachinoides*. These species feed principally on human blood; they breed in shady places by the edges of streams and water holes. Human beings are bitten and infected when they visit these streams and water holes to wash and to collect water. The public health measures which are effective, in a given local area, are three: (1) clearing away undergrowth at the edge of water; (2) sterilizing the blood of infected persons; (3) prevention of migration of infected persons into the "cleansed" area from adjacent endemic areas. The first requires continuous public attention and compliance in brush-clearing. The second requires that infected persons, or their relatives, bring cases of tryps in the early stages for chemical treatment (before the pathological sleeping and schizophrenia-like symptoms begin, and when the illness is manifested chiefly by a miscellany of somatic complaints—aches and pains, fever, headache, amenorrhea, etc.). It is difficult, however, to recognize tryps in the early stages, because its early symptoms are difficult to distinguish from both malaria and yaws, which almost everyone in the region is apt to experience at one time or another; and the later stages are similar to syphilitic paresis. The third measure requires control of immigration which is impossible for various economic and political reasons: ". . . the Gold Coast is surrounded by endemic areas and there is a virtually uncontrollable migration of persons across its borders, which are only arbitrarily defined, so that, until tryps has been eradicated from tropical Africa as a whole, epidemics and sporadic cases are bound to occur" (Tooth, 1950, p. 2). Thus, we find that the incidence of tryps is affected by a host of culturally-bound factors: the technology of water use, the availability of labor supply for brush clearing, awareness of the value of chemical treatment, economic pressures affecting migration, the location and significance of the political boundaries, various cultural factors that affect the incidence of yaws and malaria (because their incidence determines the "visibility" of early tryps), and so on.

Tryps is not an unusual example. Other "organic" psychoses—for instance, general paresis accompanying the tertiary stage of syphilis, and the mental disorders accompanying nutritional deficiencies—with equal obviousness are related to cultural factors via the mediation of the structure of sexual, economic, religious, domestic, and political relations, and of popular beliefs and attitudes relating to the disorder in question. Still other disorders, at present regarded as psychogenic, also may be caused by factors, such as nutritional and infectious disease, and thus be related indirectly, rather than directly to culture.

Culture as Direct Pathogenic Influence

WE HAVE DEFINED the "direct pathogenic influence" of culture, in respect to mental disorder, as the result of conflict-and-anxiety-producing sets of cultural forms. The reader will note that we are concerned, here, not with culture as determinant of the *content* of disorder, but of its *occurrence* and that, for the sake of simplicity of exposition, we shall not labor a point already made: that the weaknesses of the microcosmic viewpoint afflict most of the several fairly specific types of hypotheses. Most of these hypotheses which have been offered to explain the function of culture as a direct pathogenic influence are based on one variety or another of psychoanalytic theory.

(1) CULTURE PER SE AS CAUSE OF NEUROSIS Freud expressed a view, common to many a humanist, that there is an unavoidable tragedy inherent in the human condition—namely, that the practical necessity of maintaining and transmitting across generations *any* sort of culture demands the partial, but grievous, frustration of human instincts, both sexual and aggressive. Such instinctual deprivation inevitably elicits from all human beings some sort of neurotic compromise, of greater or lesser degree, ranging from such minor phenomena as slips of the tongue and selective forgetting of unpleasant experiences, to the grand symptoms of clinical neurosis. This view is embedded, of course, in larger philosophical speculations about the universality of the Oedipus complex, castration anxiety, and self-destructive tendencies. Many anthropologists, somewhat naively, object that culture is a complex device for instinctual gratification

rather than for deprivation. It is certainly true that human instincts are usually gratified, when they are gratified, in a cultural medium; but it is also true that human instincts are frustrated, when they are frustrated, in a cultural medium.

(2) CULTURE AS CONTENT OF NEUROSIS   Some anthropologists (e.g., Roheim, 1943) and anthropologically inclined psychoanalysts (e.g., Kardiner, 1939) have felt that major areas of the culture pattern of any given society may be conceived as widely shared and institutionalized neurotic, or even psychotic, symptomatology, arising out of particular instinctual deprivations imposed on the members, particularly in their childhood. ("Neurosis," in this usage, implies that various mechanisms of defense are employed in the building and maintenance of the personality structure; but since all human beings use such mechanisms, all have a "neurosis" in this generic sense.) This view does not necessarily include the doctrine that culture, per se, invariably produces neurosis, and some of these authors even offer recipes for non-neurotic cultures based on enlightened methods of child rearing. Usually, it is the so-called "projective systems"—religious belief and ritual, aspects of political relations, mythology, art, and so forth, which are believed to be related to particular systems of child rearing—to which the tag "neurotic" is applied. In incautious hands, such an approach is dangerous, for even professedly straightforward cultural or modal personality description may imply that an entire people is "sick," as when Benedict (1934) casually describes the Kwakiutl society as "megalomaniac paranoid." Such characterization of whole societies or cultures as mentally ill is rarely, if ever, defensible on scientific grounds; a society of psychotics is a contradiction in terms, and the use of a diagnostic label in national character evaluation ex-

presses merely the author's hostility toward the subjects of his description. Sometimes, of course, psychiatric terms must be used to describe mental processes which occur in both sick and healthy persons as, for instance, the terms for defense mechanisms, such as "repression," "sublimation," etc. When such descriptive langauge is used in a modal personality statement, without the use of diagnostic labels, no harm is done, unless the naive reader wrongly infers psychopathology whenever a piece of psychiatric jargon is employed. But the use of diagnostic labels, such as "paranoid," "psychotic," and "schizophrenic," or words implying such labels, is *never* justified when referring to an entire society, except in cases where that society has suffered a major and identifiable trauma to which an illness, definable by the group itself as a pathological state, is a general response. Another risk in this mode of analysis is the overly free imputation of unconscious purpose to account for functional relationships in culture. Clinical psychoanalytic interpretation depends heavily upon the guess that describing the consequences of an act will define its motives. In culture-and-personality analysis, the entire culture of a society is regarded as the consequence of the acts of its members. The statement that some pattern of unconscious motives creates and maintains the culture is apt to invoke an animistic teleology which, however useful in the art of psychotherapy, is not justifiable in rigorous analysis. Furthermore, it requires the use of the dubious "cultural-deductive method" (Wallace, 1952a).

(3) CULTURALLY ENJOINED "DISORDERS" In many societies, religious ritual and other ceremonial protocol require individuals of certain statuses to undergo types of experiences which, in contemporary Western psychiatric tradition, often are regarded as symptomatic of mental disorder. The class of pseudo-illnesses.

culturally enjoined, include such diverse phenomena as ritual dissociation (trance and possession), drug or alcohol intoxication (as, for example, in peyote), self-mortification leading to hallucination (as in the vision quest), ceremonial torture and cannibalism, and ecstatic conversion experiences. The physiological and psychological mechanisms immediately involved in the "abnormal" state in such pseudo-disorders may well be the same as those involved in symptom production in Western mental patients. Nevertheless, the consequences of such experiences are vastly different, since a "ceremonial" neurosis or psychosis, unlike the "true" disease, is voluntarily initiated, is usually reversible, and leads neither the subject nor his associates to classify him as "abnormal" and unworthy of complete social participation. Such disorders are comparable, in our own society, to the generation of dissociated states in healthy individuals by hypnosis, or the production of hallucinations by administration of lysergic acid or sensory deprivation, or the elicitation of disorganized speech in guests at a cocktail party. The subjects of such manipulations are not, as persons, classified as mentally ill, despite the fact that, under special circumstances, they have temporarily entered states which characterize chronically some mentally ill persons.

(4) CULTURAL DEFINITIONS OF THE MEANING OF "SYMPTOMS" It may be taken as axiomatic that it is the concern of all human beings to maintain an image of themselves as persons competent to attain their essential goals, including maintenance of group membership. Such a self-image in part is dependent on the individual's evaluation of his own behavior, and in part on the evaluation of this behavior which is communicated to him by others. Shame—awareness of incompetence in any sphere, whether growing from self-observation

or information from others—may arouse so much anxiety as to inhibit further the person's competence. In our own society, serious mental disease is conceived and recognized by law as a generalized incompetence and (not unexpectedly) the imputation of mental disease to an individual is a commonly used metaphor of insult. It is also popularly believed to be possible to "gaslight" a perfectly healthy person into psychosis by interpreting his own behavior to him as symptomatic of serious mental illness. While "gaslighting" itself may be a mythical crime, there is no question that any social attitude which interprets a given behavior or experience as symptomatic of a generalized incompetence is a powerful creator of shame, and thus of anxiety, in those who experience or behave in the "symptomatic" way. One may expect, then, that whenever a culture defines a given item of behavior as a symptom of general incompetence, the individual so behaving will suffer from shame, which elicits anxiety. This anxiety will further tend to decrease his competence, thus precipitating a reciprocal interaction between "incompetent" behaviors and anxiety. In one society, foci of anxiety over competence may center about sexual potency or attractiveness; in another, on courage in war; in still another, on intelligence, and so on. Furthermore, those behaviors, such as hallucination, which Western societies generally interpret as symptoms of that generalized incompetence legally known as "insanity," may be less heavily stressed, or not be stressed at all, in others (cf. Wallace, 1959). To the extent that a society stresses failure in a given area of behavior as symptomatic of a more generalized inadequacy, and to the extent that that behavior requires minimal anxiety for successful performance, failure in such behavior probably will be repeated and will increasingly extend over other behaviors. Such reciprocal processes of shame, anxiety, and incompetent behavior are recognized today in our own mental hospitals, where patients are found to respond dramatically to almost any treatment which is carried on in an atmosphere of confidence in the ability of the patient to regain competence. Mental health associations also have worked assiduously to change popular concepts of mental disease, from the stereotype of a shameful and incurable incompetency to a respectable and curable "disease like any other." Similar contrasts in social evaluation of symptomatology, and in the amount of anxiety and deterioration consequent upon them, are worthy of study in other societies.

(5) CULTURE CONFLICT AND CULTURE CHANGE
Anthropologists frequently have made note of the fact that primitive groups, who have been forced into situations of culture conflict and of partial, unorganized acculturation, seem prone to a higher frequency of the milder neurotic and personality trait disorders. Chronic anxiety and tension, psychosomatic complaints, alcoholism, narcotic addiction, delinquency and crime, witch fear, regressive or stunted personality development: such disorders apparently proliferate under the conditions produced by culture conflict and partial acculturation. Sociologists have reported that, among migrant groups (Malzberg and Lee, 1956), not only the incidence of such milder disorders, but also the incidence of psychosis, is measurably higher. We have discussed some of these phenomena already, in the chapter on the psychology of culture change. Although, as usual, statistical confirmation or disconfirmation of such a hypothesis is difficult to achieve, the position that culture change is associated with mental disorder has a certain obvious plausibility. But it must not be imagined that mere change in itself is so powerful a determinant that

it will elicit sharply increasing incidences of psychosis. Goldhamer and Marshall (1953), for instance, studied the trends in incidence of institutionalized psychosis in America, over a hundred year period, and found that the rate of psychosis has remained constant, despite the accelerating rate of cultural change. There is, however, one socio-cultural characteristic seemingly shared by all groups which display a markedly high general incidence of mental disorders and which is often associated with culture conflict and culture change. That characteristic is relatively low social status in the larger society of which the group is a part. Semi-primitive peoples, living on the shabby fringes of Western civilization, migrants in new lands, occupants of slum areas, and lower racial, ethnic, and socio-economic classes, generally, are characterized by high incidences of both neurosis and psychosis. This suggests that a combination of physical disadvantages, such as inadequate diet, and of the reciprocal process, discussed in the preceding section of social incompetence, shame, and anxiety, may be major factors influencing the incidence of both the psychotic and the neurotic diseases.

(6) STRESSES PRODUCED BY ROLE AND VALUE CONFLICTS IMPLICIT IN PARTICULAR SOCIO-CULTUR L SYSTEMS Many social scientists have sought to combine epidemiological data and processual theory by the use of formulations which interpret each culture as presenting to the individual a unique spectrum of highly probable stress situations; these are determined by role or value conflicts implicit in the culture. From this standpoint, a particular socio-cultural system is conceived as a congeries of roles and values, with each individual during the course of his life assuming several of these roles, some of them successively and some simultaneously, and likewise addressing himself to a number of different val-

ues, depending on the occasion. Such culture conflict
can be of two kinds: role incompatibility, and value incompatibility. Whenever an individual is put in a position where two incompatible roles must be played simultaneously, he experiences stress, since he cannot succeed
in both. And whenever an individual, playing one role,
is faced with a situation where successful performance
with respect to one value entails a high likelihood of personal loss (e.g., death) with respect to another, he experiences stress. Role incompatibility conflicts can be
further divided into two sub-types: conflicts centering
about role replacement, and conflicts centering about
simultaneous roles. Role replacement means the drop-
ping of one role for another; such events in the life cycle
as birth, weaning, puberty, marriage, birth of child, re-
tirement, and so on, frequently celebrated by *rites de
passage,* are common examples of role replacement.
Since role replacement entails loss of previously enjoyed
rewards, the individual is apt to suffer the double stress
of deprivation of past rewards and of fear of punishment if such rewards are sought again via the discon-
tinued role. Role simultaneity conflicts are less easily
noticeable, presumably because they are consciously
pruned away in most societies as productive of both
individual and social disturbance; at least they are
avoided by scheduling role performance, so as to prevent conflict, and by defining roles hierarchically, according to the relative importance of their goals. Such
conflicts do, however, frequently emerge in unanticipated situations where one or another event has inter-
fered with the normal scheduling of role behavior. This
is illustrated in the role conflicts experienced by civil
defense personnel during natural and man-made disasters. Another well-known category of role simultaneity
conflict is provided by the phenomenon of "conflict of

interest" in political organization. Value incompatibility conflicts are, again, not usually part of the ideal design of a culture, and societies attempt to forestall them by elaborate training. The classic—and an almost universal —example of value incompatibility conflicts is associated with the role of the warrior or soldier who must constantly make the choice between, in effect, being a live coward and a dead hero. Role and value conflict situations seem peculiarly apt to elicit neurotic responses; for example, in "combat fatigue" or "shell shock"; in fugues, amnesias, and a variety of phobic and neurotic compromise symptoms, in which one response to the situation is repressed, often only to be allowed to return in disguised or distorted form. It may be questioned, however, whether such situations, culturally determined insofar as the content of the conflict is determined, are to be regarded as responsible for more than the superficial content of psychoses. Psychosis, in this context, is perhaps better regarded as the result of a cognitive inability to respond neurotically to a situation in which a neurotic response is the only way the "normal" individual has of avoiding a display of gross incompetence, with its consequent and crippling shame and anxiety cycle.

(7) THE "BAD MOTHER" THEORY A special form of the internalized conflict theory has received emphasis recently in the work of psychiatrists, psychologists, and social scientists who seek to find in the parent-child, and especially the mother-child, relationship the etiology of schizophrenia. According to this view, the nuclear process in schizophrenia is withdrawal, both physical and psychological, from a world which has bombarded the victim with inconsistent communications —communications which demanded that he perform mutually incompatible roles or devote himself to anti-

thetical values. The "schizophrenogenic" mother, for example, is supposedly prone to convey the two contradictory messages, by means of kinesic as well as linguistic communication, that her child simultaneously is loved and is rejected. The child may also be explicitly ordered to play the role of "love mommy," but be subtly rejected as unworthy or offensive when he does try to play this role. This viewpoint has received a variety of theoretical formulations, from Melanie Klein's and others' postulation of antithetical "good mother-bad mother" images (cf. Bellak, 1958), to Bateson's recent attempt to construe such ambivalent mother-child relationships as a confusion of different logical types (the "double bind" hypothesis) (Bateson *et al.*, 1956). These and other attempts to construct formal models of schizophrenogenic family structures and communication systems are, however, in this writer's opinion, based on a somewhat sandy logical foundation. Most people, in most cultures, have to put up with a great deal of ambivalence and inconsistency in their social relationships; the "normal" response to extreme degrees of message inconsistency is neurotic rather than psychotic. Inability to cope with such poorly organized information suggests an inadequate capacity for organizing the data of experience.

(8) "THE MADNESS OF CROWDS"   We have already taken note of the phenomenon of culturally patterned induction of mental states which, in Western psychiatric tradition, are regarded as pathological. A related phenomenon is the affliction of groups of closely intercommunicating people with beliefs leading to culturally *in*appropriate acts. Examples of such events are mass panics, group delusions and illusions, mass hysterias, and mob violence. Such events depend, apparently, on two factors: first, the presence of a situational

context, specifically appropriate for the particular outbreak (as, for example, a locally unavoidable threat and a limited escape route, for flight panic); second, the dissociating effect on the individual of repetitive mass suggestion in a crowd, each of whose members is suggesting to several others (as, for example, in the "chain-reaction" of mounting hostility and carelessness for legal norms in a lynch mob). Such phenomena are, in a sense, acultural: the behavior of a "mad" crowd generally violates individually held, but culturally acceptable, norms. Nevertheless, the culture may indirectly determine their incidence by providing more or fewer occasions pre-suited to their occurrence. Fire panics in crowded theaters and night-clubs depend, for instance, on a host of cultural factors involved in the technology of entertainment, on architecture, and fire safety regulations. But a more direct determination is provided by the character of the group itself, as it is conceived by its individual members. Disciplined, organized groups with high morale, i.e., with the confidence of each individual in the orderliness and mutual loyalty of his fellows, do not readily experience panic or other hysterical mass dissociations, even under extreme provocation.

CULTURE AS DIRECT AND INDIRECT THERAPEUTIC AND PREVENTIVE INFLUENCE

IN THIS SECTION we shall be concerned with the therapeutic and preventive measures specifically intended by members of a community to prevent or improve mental states conceived as undesirable by the victim or his community. These mental states need not be defined by the community as "illnesses" in anything like the Western psychiatric sense, although one or another of them may be in a given society; often, in primitive societies,

psychiatric illnesses are interpreted according to a religious or magical theory, but the undesirability of leaving the sufferer or the community in an uncomfortable
condition is not questioned. Certainly some and probably all human cultures include, as part of their traditional lore, a "theory of mind" which explains such phenomena as motivation, memory, emotion, dreams and
visions, and various states which are conceived as abnormal, or at least undesirable, if continued too long.
Therapeutic measures, however originated, in general
would seem to be rationalized by such native theories.
The Iroquois Indians, for example, used a clearly articulated type of "psychoanalytic" theory to account for
dreams, obsessions, various obviously pathological behaviors, and even certain physical complaints (Wallace,
1958b). The therapeutic devices employed in the treatment of mental disorders in any society are cultural
artifacts like any others; thus, these devices are functions
not merely of the characteristics of the disease, but also
of the structure and functioning of the rest of the culture.

(1) CATHARTIC STRATEGIES   The efficacy of
occasional or periodic release of suppressed impulses
in reducing anxiety and tension is widely recognized.
Most cultures provide for some sort of "recreative"
catharsis on a periodic basis, encouraging the individual
at these stated occasions to act out wishes whose realization would be undesirable on other occasions. Saturna-
lian cathartic festivals, in which large numbers of persons participate in sexual relations disallowed at other
times, tend to attract attention as "orgies." But catharsis
is not necessarily orgiastic, it is not necessarily sexual,
and it may be either crudely direct or subtly sublimated.
Thus, a very wide range of behaviors of a recreational
character serves the function of socially encouraged ca-

tharsis: the arts (music, drama, painting, etc.), games and sports, exercise, hobbies, "sight-seeing," feasts and parties, intoxication, mourning rituals, ceremonial torture, and so on, *ad infinitum*. Seasonal variations in the pace of economic activity, diurnal cycles of fatigue and vigor, rest-days and vacations, and other time-scheduling frames of reference, are employed to permit cathartic acting out of wishes denied fulfilment in the work-a-day world. Such strategies may be rationalized in various ways, of course, depending on the local theory of mind: as means of limiting fatigue, as devices for gratifying the gods, as methods of satisfying the needs of the body, and so on. And their institutional locus may be correspondingly religious, or domestic, or medical, or whatever. The important common feature is the explicit provision of occasion for gratifying motives which cannot be gratified in the course of playing routine economic, military, domestic, or other socially necessary roles.

(2) THE INSTITUTIONAL BINDING OF ANXIETY IN COMPROMISE FORMATIONS   In the preceding section on cultural pathogenesis, it was noted that the so-called "projective systems"—particularly religious ritual, myth, and belief—by some were considered as the quasi-pathological products of culturally stereotyped childhood traumata. From a standpoint of "teleological functionalism" (Spiro, 1952), such "projective systems" may be regarded as devices which successfully bind the anxieties, originally produced by the traumata, to a restricted and socially acceptable sphere of expression by providing a patterned quasi-neurotic symptomatology. Thus, whatever the observer's evaluation of the projective system's over-all value in the general functioning of the society, it may be considered at least to have the function of preventing crippling anxiety and its expression in symptoms which might seriously interfere with the necessary

performance of various economic, sexual, political, and other roles. It might be expected that interference with the routine performance of the projective systems—in culture-change situations, for example—would be productive of severe anxiety, and either would lead to outbreaks of neurotic symptomatology of kinds destructive of the social order or to the rapid development of new projective systems by religious cults. Such a relationship has been cited as one of the factors responsible for the dual phenomena of delinquency (alcoholism, violence, sexual promiscuity, etc.), and of the innumerable separatist churches among de-tribalized African natives who are unable to continue the practice of native ritual in labor compounds and urban ghettos. Many primitive societies provide an additional resource for the individual who, for one reason or another, does not find relief in the available projective system. This is the process of "becoming a shaman" which is but one example of the process of mazeway resynthesis. The latter is a rather sudden reorganization—often but not necessarily via the medium of hallucinatory experience—of values, attitudes, and beliefs which "make sense" of a hitherto confusing and anxiety-provoking world. We discussed mazeway resynthesis earlier, as a source of cultural innovation, and pointed out then that its function for the individual was psycho-therapeutic. The therapeutic value of such an experience, however, depends both on the resources of the individual and on the support his effort is given by the community. The culture enters into the process here, rather evidently, by imposing certain evaluations on the content of such experiences, as well as on their form. Some socio-cultural systems embrace a wide range of mazeway resyntheses, sometimes by giving them the status of *rites de passage* (as in the vision quest), sometimes by effectively molding them (as in the process of becoming a shaman), and sometimes by holding open, as it were, a status for the religious innovator (as in the case of the Iroquois who encouraged private medicine societies based on the vision) or prophet (as in ancient Judaism). Other systems, like that of the American urban middle-class today, generally take a dim view of any sort of fervent personality transformation, especially if it is accompanied by hallucination. Thus, the existing cultural milieu can act as a support or a hindrance to the mazeway resynthesis process by facilitating or suppressing the institutionalization of behavior patterns and beliefs conceived in the course of such experiences.

(3) CONTROL STRATEGIES   There is reason to suspect that relatively secure and confident social groups favor cathartic strategies, but that insecure and disillusioned groups favor control strategies when dealing with mental disorders (Wallace, 1960a). The reason for a tendency of disadvantaged groups to favor control therapy presumably would lie in the fact that such groups already are faced with difficulties in practical adaptation and in maintenance of orderly social life. Under such circumstances, granting persons who already contribute to social disorganization the privilege of adding additional unpredictabilities in the course of carthartic acting out simply places added burdens on the group; furthermore, the sick person in such groups may have a greater need to perceive a better organized world. Thus, the condition of the society should favor the use of measures designed to press the deviant to exercise his "will" to control his disorders of behavior. Techniques for accomplishing this generally depend upon what we have earlier referred to as "hysterical conversion." Sermons depicting the terrors of hellfire, mass rallies, compulsory confession and penance, "thought reform" induced by

a combination of threat, confession, and indoctrination, continuous moral exhortation and encouragement, instruction conveyed symbolically in *rites de passage*—devices such as these are more effective in inducing marked "improvement" in behavior in demoralized populations than is mere threat of punishment for delinquency. Nor should it be supposed that such measures, crude though they may seem to psychiatrically sophisticated workers, are of merely superficial value. Therapeutic changes, so induced, may be remarkably stable (as in the case of the control of drunkenness among the Iroquois who joined Handsome Lake's movement). It has been argued theoretically that "super-ego reinforcement" is more effective than many cathartically oriented psychiatrists have recognized. In the military services, the newer "combat psychiatry," which combines brief (a day or two) periods of rest and verbal catharsis with reinforcement by suggestion of the victim's sense of responsibility, has been found to be much more successful in rehabilitating psychiatric casualties than conventional psychotherapy and psychoanalysis.

(4) HOSPITAL STUDIES   A growing number of anthropologists have taken part with sociologists and social psychologists in the investigation of various aspects of the cultural traditions and social structures of mental hospitals in England and America, with the ultimate view of discovering how the hospital milieu functions to promote or retard therapeutic progress. Some evidence now exists to suggest that the hospital's functioning, apart from the application of specific treatments (such as psychotherapy, electroshock, or drugs), can have a considerable effect on patient progress. Unhappily, such evidence is not very "hard": that is to say, it is rarely possible to prove that a given observed sociocultural feature of a hospital or rehabilitation unit is, to

any ascertainable degree, associated with a definite mental status in patients of a definable type (cf. Wallace and Rashkis, 1959). Thus, for instance, Henry (1954) points out that the system of "multiple subordination," characteristic of hospital social structure, maintains various chronic stresses on the nursing staff. But it is not easy to show that multiple subordination is responsible for a significantly higher or lower rate of patient progress, other things being equal, in comparison with any other hypothesized system of hospital management. Furthermore, evaluation of therapy is a difficult task for the technically untrained observer. Indeed, in view of the uncertainty of the state of knowledge about the kinds of treatment processes which are "good" and "bad" for patients anyway, and in view of the multiplicity of influences to which every patient is subjected, little more can be expected at present than the somewhat random collection of data and suggestions. These are made in the hope of coming across factors which can be shown to have a major impact on particular types of patients under definable circumstances.

THE IMPACT OF MENTAL ILLNESS ON CULTURE

UP TO THIS POINT we have been considering primarily the ways in which culturally standardized measures operate to cause, treat, or prevent mental disorder. Now we shall briefly examine the reciprocal effect: the ways in which mental disorder, or the fear of mental disorder, determine the nature and manner of functioning of the culture.

The fulcrum of such a causal relation is the "cost" of illness. Such costs may or may not be correctly perceived, or be consciously perceived at all, by the members of the society. Nevertheless, they are present, as interferences with the operation of institutions and, thus, as barriers between the group and the achievement of the values toward which its members strive. Some such costs are irremediable: mental illness simply functions in the societal calculus as a kind of internal waste factor. Such wastage is, in our own society, rationally calculated in terms of dollars and cents spent for medical care and of man hours lost in the labor market. It has been estimated that mental illness in the United States costs about $3,000,000,000 per year (Fein, 1958). Such indices only approximately represent other, less readily countable, costs, levied on society via the contribution of mental illness to crime, delinquency, accident, family disorganization, and relative inefficiency in innumerable tasks.

Costs of mental illness are observable in non-industrial societies. Tooth (1950, pp. 1-2), evaluating the "sociological" impact of *Trypanosomiasis* in West Africa, makes the following trenchant commentary:

> In endemic districts the frequency of the disease may have a profound influence on the lives of the population; the effects may be clearly seen by correlating the vital statistics and the movements of the population with the incidence of infection. But the disorganising effects on smaller units of the community are not so generally appreciated. Apart from the reduction of efficiency and reproductive capacity due to the physical factors, psychological changes have their repercussions in the home, the schools and the Courts. In a social organisation where divorce is relatively easy, the change of character of one of the partners of a marriage frequently leads to the break-up of the home or, at least, to the formation of a most unfavourable atmosphere for the upbringing of the children. Misbehavior and backwardness in school, unless it is recognised as a symptom of illness, can not only cause

unhappiness to the children themselves but is also a waste of valuable time and public money; the demand for education is so great that the failure of a pupil to complete the course is a serious matter. There is little doubt that Tryps. is a not uncommon cause of delinquency in children and crime in adults; the police and administrative authorities are aware of this but, in the absence of any gross pathological changes, it may be very difficult for a medical officer unfamiliar with the clinical variations, to express a convincing opinion that disease is the cause of the misconduct. Another not inconsiderable social factor is the existence of advanced and incurable Tryps. dements living as beggars in the towns and taking up space in mental institutions which could be better used for the treatment of recoverable causes of mental illness.

There is no reason to suppose that similar observations could not be made about the consequences of any prevalent mental disorder in any society, primitive or civilized. One also may draw attention to the fact that mental disorders, when they exist in persons who, for one reason or another, occupy strategic decision-making positions in the political structure, may bring about trains of consequences so catastrophic as to magnify the costs of illness to a level which threatens the survival of whole societies.

We have already spoken of the measures which societies take to treat or prevent mental disorder. When such measures fail, and the disorder is too costly to be tolerated, all societies have recourse to a more primitive device: the extrusion of the mentally sick person from the community in order to protect the community. This may, of course, be accomplished by killing him, after defining him as an enemy or criminal; but, more commonly, the victim is forcibly restrained from social participation while he is maintained alive. In our own society, when a person is declared to be legally insane (i.e., a potential danger to himself and/or others), he is incarcerated in a mental hospital where he may, or may not, be given treatment. In the absence of hospitals, the socially disruptive person is physically restrained by any convenient device: by being chained to a heavy log; by being confined in a cage; by tying with ropes, and so on. Such restraint is removed when the sick person ceases to exhibit his threatening symptoms.

The more subtle "cost," however, of mental illness, probably resides in the gradual warping of cultures as they undergo changes whose function (not necessarily intention) is to minimize socially disruptive symptomatology (such as physical aggression, suicide, incest, etc.). Such warping is difficult to recognize and evaluate (since it invokes the problem of the cultural relativity of conceptions of what a "good" culture is). To the aggressively intellectual and materialistic scientist, religious customs which function to minimize mental disorders by institutionalizing them in innocuous "symptoms" appear to be too high a price to pay. To the more humanistic, and less ethnocentric, scientist, this warping hardly seems to be as high a price as such heroic measures as the compulsory sterilization of "defectives" recommended by genetically minded demagogues, or the assumption of responsibility for mental health by social control and education agencies. Whatever the optimum strategy for minimizing the cost of mental illness may be for any particular society, however, the problem is a universal one and a solution is devised by every culture.

Conclusion

THE FOREGOING PAGES have critically reviewed a number of concepts and theories which have been important in the development of the anthropological sub-discipline of culture-and-personality. It has been argued here that the true function of the culture-and-personality approach in anthropology lies not in its ability to provide such descriptions of the psychological correlates of culture—"ethos," "modal personality," "values," "world-view," and so on—as will make a kind of humanistic frosting on the scientific cake. Rather, it is suggested that culture-and-personality recognizes that culture is an open system and that, without culture-and-personality to connect it to the rest of science, culturology can only blunder into one of those sterile wastelands where all closed-system theories eventually end their days. Culture-and-personality takes the documented facts of cultural evolution, culture change, and cultural diversity as the phenomena to be explained; but in explanation it is—as all scientific explanations must be—unashamedly reductionistic. It seeks to describe in individuals the classes of micro-phenomena which are the parameters of the classes of macro-phenomena which the pure culturologist describes for groups. In so doing, its traditional concentration on psychoanalytically based theory is being increasingly combined with attention to biological variables. For "human nature" is far from being a constant parameter of cultural events; indeed, the biological mechanism upon which culture depends is exquisitely variable in response to genetic and ecological processes which, in part, are radically independent of culture per se. And the culture-and-personality viewpoint is also being broadened to encompass more than the study of affect and motivation and their determinants; greater importance is being given to cognitive, even "rational," processes (which are, incidentally, also receiving increasing attention from contemporary psychology).

In the next generation, indeed, we may expect to see graduate students in cultural anthropology who are aware that every human being has, in addition to his culture and his personality, both a body and a brain.

Bibliography

Aberle, David F., Cohen, A., Davis, A., Levy, M., and Sutton, F. 1950. "The Functional Prerequisites of a Society." *Ethics*, 60:100-111.

American Psychiatric Association. 1952. *Diagnostic and Statistical Manual: Mental Disorders*. Washington.

Ames, Michael M. 1957. "Reaction to Stress: A Comparative Study of Nativism." *Davidson Journal of Anthropology*, 3:17-30.

Angel, J. Lawrence. 1960. "Physical and Psychological Factors in Culture Growth." In Anthony F. C. Wallace, ed., *Selected Papers of the Fifth International Congress of Anthropological and Ethnological Sciences* (Philadelphia: University of Pennsylvania Press).

Barnett, H. G. 1953. *Innovation: The Basis of Cultural Change*. New York: McGraw-Hill.

Bateson, Gregory, *et al.* 1956. "Toward a Theory of Schizophrenia." *Behavioral Science*, 1:251-264.

Beaglehole, Ernest. 1949. "Cultural Complexity and Psychological Problems." In Patrick Mullahy, ed., *A Study of Interpersonal Relations* (New York: Hermitage House).

Bellak, Leopold. 1958. *Schizophrenia: A Review of the Syndrome.* New York: Logos Press.

Belo, Jane. 1935. "The Balinese Temper." *Character and Personality,* 4:120-146.

Benedict, Paul K., and Jacks, Irving. 1954. "Mental Illness in Primitive Societies." *Psychiatry,* 17:377-389.

Benedict, Ruth. 1934. *Patterns of Culture.* Boston: Houghton Mifflin.

————. 1938. "Continuities and Discontinuities in Cultural Conditioning." *Psychiatry,* 1:161-167.

Bidney, David. 1953. *Theoretical Anthropology.* New York: Columbia University Press.

Birdwhistell, Raymond N. 1952. "Body Motion Research and Interviewing." *Human Organization,* 11:37-38.

Boulding, Kenneth E. 1956. *The Image.* Ann Arbor: University of Michigan Press.

Bury, J. B. 1921. *The Idea of Progress.* London: Macmillan.

Cassirer, Ernst. 1946. *Language and Myth.* New York: Dover.

Chomsky, Naom. 1959. Review of *Verbal Behavior* by B. F. Skinner. *Language,* 35:26-58.

Conant, James B. 1951. *On Understanding Science.* New York: New American Library.

Coon, Carleton S. 1948. *A Reader in General Anthropology.* New York: Holt, Rinehart, Winston.

————. 1950. "Human Races in Relation to Environment and Culture with Special Reference to the Influence of Culture upon Genetic Changes in the Human Population." In *Origin and Evolution of Man* (Cold Spring Harbor, N.Y.: Symposia on Quantitative Biology, Vol. 15).

Count, Earl W. 1958. "The Biological Basis of Human Sociality." *American Anthropologist,* 60:1049-1085.

Devereux, George. 1956. "Normal and Abnormal: The Key Problem of Psychiatric Anthropology." In *Some Uses of Anthropology, Theoretical and Applied* (Washington: Anthropological Society of Washington).

Dobzhansky, Theodosius. 1955. *Evolution, Genetics, and Man.* New York: Wiley. Copyright, 1955, by John Wiley and Sons, Inc.

———. 1956. "Does Natural Selection Continue to Operate in Modern Mankind?" *American Anthropologist,* 58:591-604.

DuBois, Cora. 1944. *The People of Alor.* Minneapolis: University of Minnesota Press.

Durkheim, Emile. n.d. *The Elementary Forms of the Religious Life.* London: Allen & Unwin.

Edinger, Tilly. 1948. *Evolution of the Horse Brain.* Geological Society of America, Memoir 25.

Eiseley, Loren C. 1958. *Darwin's Century: Evolution and the Men Who Discovered It.* New York: Doubleday. Copyright © 1958 by Loren C. Eiseley. Reprinted by permission of Doubleday and Company, Inc.

Etkin, William. 1954. "Social Behavior and the Evolution of Man's Mental Faculties." *American Naturalist,* 88: 129-142.

Fein, Rashi. 1958. *Economics of Mental Illness.* New York: Basic Books.

Festinger, Leon. 1957. *A Theory of Cognitive Dissonance.* Evanston, Ill.: Row, Peterson.

Gerard, Ralph, Kluckhohn, Clyde, and Rapoport, Anatol. 1956. "Biological and Cultural Evolution: Some Analogies and Explorations." *Behavioral Science,* 1:6-34.

Goldhamer, H., and Marshall, A. 1953. *Psychosis and Civilization.* Glencoe, Ill.: Free Press.

Goodenough, Ward H. 1956. "Componential Analysis and the Study of Meaning." *Language,* 32:195-216.

———. n.d. *Cooperation in Change.* In preparation.

Gorer, G., and Rickman, J. 1949. *The People of Great Russia*. London: Cresset Press.

Hallowell, A. Irving. 1950. "Personality Structure and the Evolution of Man." *American Anthropologist,* 52: 159-174.

———. 1954. "Psychology and Anthropology." In John Gillin, ed., *For a Science of Social Man* (New York: Macmillan).

———. 1955. *Culture and Experience*. Philadelphia: University of Pennsylvania Press.

———. 1956. "The Structural and Functional Dimensions of a Human Existence." *Quarterly Review of Biology,* 31:88-101.

———. 1959. "Behavioral Evolution and the Emergence of the Self." In *Evolution and Anthropology: A Centennial Appraisal* (Washington, D.C.: The Anthropological Society of Washington).

Haring, Douglas (ed.). 1956. *Personal Character and Cultural Milieu: A Collection of Readings*. 3rd edition. New York: Syracuse University Press.

Hayes, Keith J., and Hayes, Catharine. 1955. "The Cultural Capacity of Chimpanzees." In James A. Gavan, ed., *The Non-Human Primates and Human Evolution* (Detroit: Wayne University Press).

Henry, Jules. 1954. "The Formal Social Structure of a Psychiatric Hospital." *Psychiatry,* 17:139-151.

———. 1959. "Culture, Personality, and Evolution." *American Anthropologist,* 61:221-226.

Henry, Jules, and Spiro, Melford E. 1953. "Psychological Techniques: Projective Tests in Field Work." In A. L. Kroeber, ed. *Anthropology Today* (Chicago: University of Chicago Press).

Herskovits, Melville. 1948. *Man and His Works*. New York: Knopf.

Hess, E. H. 1959. "Imprinting." *Science,* 130:133-141.

Hodgen, Margaret T. 1952. *Change and History*. New York: Wenner-Gren Foundation.

Honigmann, John J. 1954. *Culture and Personality*. New York: Harper.

Hsu, Francis L. K. 1952. "Anthropology or Psychiatry: A Definition of Objectives and Their Implications." *Southwestern Journal of Anthropology*, 8:227-250.

———— (ed.). 1954. *Aspects of Culture and Personality: A Symposium*. New York: Abelard-Schuman.

Huxley, Julian. 1941. *Man Stands Alone*. New York: Harper.

————. 1955. "Evolution, Cultural and Biological." In William L. Thomas, Jr., ed., *Current Anthropology: A Supplement to Anthropology Today* (Chicago: University of Chicago Press. Copyright 1955 by the University of Chicago).

Inkeles, Alex. 1954. "National Character: The Study of Modal Personality and Socio-cultural Systems." In G. Lindzey, ed., *Handbook of Social Psychology*, Vol. 2 (Cambridge, Mass.: Addison-Wesley).

Jahoda, Marie. 1958. *Current Concepts of Positive Mental Health*. New York: Basic Books.

Jerison, Harry J. 1955. "Brain to Body Ratios and the Evolution of Intelligence." *Science*, 121:447-449.

Kallman, Franz J. 1938. *The Genetics of Schizophrenia*. New York: J. J. Augustin.

Kaplan, Bert. 1957. "Personality and Social Structure." In J. B. Gittler, ed., *Review of Sociology: Analysis of a Decade* (New York: Wiley).

Kardiner, Abram. 1939. *The Individual and His Society*. New York: Columbia University Press.

————. 1945. *The Psychological Frontiers of Society*. New York: Columbia University Press.

Kardiner, Abram, and Ovesey, Lionel. 1951. *The Mark of Oppression*. New York: Norton.

Kelleher, Roger T. 1958. "Concept Formation in Chimpanzees." *Science,* 128:777-778.

Kety, S. S. 1959. "Biochemical Theories of Schizophrenia." *Science,* 129:1528-1532, 1590-1596.

Klineberg, Otto. 1938. "Emotional Expression in Chinese Literature." *Journal of Abnormal and Social Psychology,* 33:517-520.

Kluckhohn, Clyde. 1944. "The Influence of Psychiatry on Anthropology in America During the Past One Hundred Years." In J. K. Hall, G. Zilboorg, and H. A. Bunker, eds., *One Hundred Years of American Psychiatry* (New York: Columbia University Press).

———. 1954. "Culture and Behavior." In G. Lindzey, ed., *Handbook of Social Psychology,* Vol. 2 (Cambridge, Mass.: Addison-Wesley).

Kluckhohn, Clyde, Murray, Henry A., and Schneider, David M. (eds.). 1953. *Personality in Nature, Society, and Culture.* 2nd ed. New York: Knopf.

Kroeber, A. L. 1917. "The Superorganic." *American Anthropologist,* 19 (No. 2).

———. 1939. *Cultural and Natural Areas of Native North America.* Berkeley and Los Angeles: University of California Press.

———. 1944. *Configurations of Culture Growth.* Berkeley and Los Angeles: University of California Press.

———. 1948. *Anthropology.* New York: Harcourt, Brace.

LaBarre, Weston. 1955. *The Human Animal.* Chicago: University of Chicago Press.

———. 1958. "The Influence of Freud on Anthropology." *American Imago,* 15:275-328.

Lessa, William A., and Spiegelman, Marvin. 1954. *Ulithian Personality as Seen Through Ethnological Materials and Thematic Test Analysis.* Berkeley: University of California Press.

Linton, Ralph. 1936. *The Study of Man*. New York: D. Appleton-Century. By permission of Appleton-Century-Crofts, Inc. Copyright, 1936, D. Appleton-Century Co.

———. 1945. *The Cultural Background of Personality*. New York: Appleton-Century-Crofts.

———. 1947. "The Change from Dry to Wet Rice Culture in Tanala-Betsileo." In T. M. Newcomb and E. L. Hartley, eds., *Readings in Social Psychology* (New York: Holt, Rinehart, Winston).

———. 1956. *Culture and Mental Disorders*. Springfield, Ill.: Thomas.

Lindesmith, Alfred R., and Strauss, Anselm L. 1950. "A Critique of Culture-Personality Writings." *American Sociological Review*, 15:587-600.

Lounsbury, Floyd G. 1956. "A Semantic Analysis of the Pawnee Kinship Usage." *Language*, 32:158-194.

Löwith, Karl. 1949. *Meaning in History*. Chicago: University of Chicago Press.

Malzberg, Benjamin, and Lee, E. S. 1956. *Migration and Mental Disease*. New York: Social Science Research Council.

Mandelbaum, David G. (ed.). 1949. *Selected Writings of Edward Sapir*. Berkeley: University of California Press.

Mannheim, Karl. 1936. *Ideology and Utopia*. New York: Harcourt, Brace.

Mead, George H. 1934. *Mind, Self, and Society*. Chicago: University of Chicago Press.

Mead, Margaret. 1947a. "The Concept of Culture and the Psychosomatic Approach." *Psychiatry*, 10:57-76.

———. 1947b. "The Implications of Culture Change for Personality Development." *American Journal of Orthopsychiatry*, 17:633-646.

———. 1953. "National Character." In A. L. Kroeber, ed., *Anthropology Today* (Chicago: University of Chicago Press).

————. 1955. *Cultural Patterns and Technical Change*. New York: New American Library.

————. 1956. *New Lives for Old*. New York: Morrow.

Mead, Margaret, and Metraux, Rhoda (eds.). 1953. *The Study of Culture at a Distance*. Chicago: University of Chicago Press. Copyright 1953 by the University of Chicago.

Miller, George, Galanter, E., and Pribram, K. 1960. *Plans and the Structure of Behavior*. New York: Holt, Rinehart, Winston.

Montagu, M. F. Ashley, and Dobzhansky, Theodosius. 1947. "Natural Selection and the Mental Capacities of Mankind." *Science,* 105:587-590.

Murdock, George P. 1949. *Social Structure*. New York: Macmillan.

Oakley, Kenneth. 1955. "Fire as Paleolithic Tool and Weapon." *Proceedings of the Prehistoric Society,* 21: 36-48.

Opler, Marvin. 1956. *Culture, Psychiatry, and Human Values*. Springfield, Ill.: Thomas.

Opler, Marvin, and Singer, J. L. 1956. "Contrasting Patterns of Fantasy and Mobility in Irish and Italian Schizophrenics." *Journal of Abnormal and Social Psychology,* 53:42-47.

Opler, Morris. 1945. "Themes as Dynamic Forces in Culture." *American Journal of Sociology,* 51:198-206.

Orlansky, Harold. 1949. "Infant Care and Personality." *Psychological Bulletin,* 46:1-48.

Osgood, Charles E., Suchi, George J., and Tannenbaum, Percy H. 1957. *The Measurement of Meaning*. Urbana: University of Illinois Press.

Parsons, Talcott, and Shils, Edward (eds.). 1952. *Toward a General Theory of Action*. Cambridge: Harvard University Press.

Paul, Benjamin D. (ed.). 1955. *Health, Culture, and Community: Case Studies of Public Reactions to Health Programs*. New York: Russell Sage Foundation.

Pettitt, George A. 1946. *Primitive Education in North America*. Berkeley and Los Angeles: University of California Press.

Rapoport, Robert N. 1954. *Changing Navaho Religious Values*. Cambridge, Mass.: Peabody Museum of American Archaeology and Ethnology, Harvard University.

Rashkis, Harold A. 1957. "A General Theory of Treatment in Psychiatry." *A.M.A. Archives of Neurology and Psychiatry*, 78:491-499.

Redfield, Robert. 1952. "The Primitive World View." *Proceedings of the American Philosophical Society*, 96:30-36.

————. 1953. *The Primitive World and Its Transformations*. Ithaca, N.Y.: Cornell University Press.

Reina, Ruben. 1958. "Political Crisis and Revitalization: The Guatemalan Case." *Human Organization*, 17:14-18.

Riesman, David. 1950. *The Lonely Crowd: A Study of the Changing American Character*. New Haven: Yale University Press.

Roheim, Geza. 1943. *The Origin and Function of Culture*. New York: Nervous and Mental Disease Monographs, No. 69.

Sapir, Edward. See Mandelbaum, David G.

Sarason, Seymour B., and Gladwin, Thomas. 1958. *Psychological and Cultural Problems in Mental Subnormality: A Review of Research*. Genetic Psychology Monographs, No. 57.

Sahlins, Marshall D., and Service, Elman R. (eds.). 1960. *Evolution and Culture*. Ann Arbor: University of Michigan Press.

Sargant, S. Stansfeld, and Smith, Marian W. (eds.). 1949. *Culture and Personality*. New York: Viking Fund.

Sargant, William. 1957. *Battle for the Mind*. New York: Doubleday.

Scheerer, Martin. 1954. "Cognitive Theory." In G. Lindzey, ed., *Handbook of Social Psychology* Vol. 1 (Cambridge, Mass.: Addison-Wesley).

Schilder, Paul. 1935. *The Image and Appearance of the Human Body*. London: Kegan Paul, and Trench, Trubner.

Schultz, Adolph H. 1950. "The Specializations of Man and His Place among the Catarrhine Primates." In *Origin and Evolution of Man* (Cold Spring Harbor, N.Y.: Symposia on Quantitative Biology, Vol. 15).

Sewell, William H. 1952. "Infant-Training and the Personality of the Child." *American Journal of Sociology, 58*: 150-159.

Simpson, George G. 1949. *The Meaning of Evolution*. New Haven: Yale University Press.

Spicer, Edward H. 1952. *Human Problems in Technological Change*. New York: Russell Sage Foundation.

Spindler, George D. 1955. *Sociocultural and Psychological Processes in Menominee Acculturation*. Berkeley and Los Angeles: University of California Press.

Spiro, Melford E. 1951. "Culture and Personality: The Natural History of a False Dichotomy." *Psychiatry, 14*: 19-46.

―――. 1952. "Ghosts, Ifaluk, and Teleological Functionalism." *American Anthropologist, 54*:497-503.

―――. 1954. "Human Nature in Its Psychological Dimensions." *American Anthropologist, 56*:19-30.

Spuhler, J. N. (ed.). 1959. *The Evolution of Man's Capacity for Culture*. Detroit: Wayne State University Press.

Tappen, Neil C. 1953. "A Mechanistic Theory of Human Evolution." *American Anthropologist, 55*:605-607.

Tolman, E. D. 1948. "Cognitive Maps in Rats and Men." *Psychological Review, 55*:189-208.

Tooth, Geoffrey. 1950. *Studies in Mental Illness in the Gold Coast*. London: H. M. Stationery Office.

Tylor, Edward B. 1900. *Anthropology*. New York: Appleton-Century-Croft.

Wallace, Anthony F. C. 1951. "Some Psychological Determinants of Culture Change in an Iroquoian Community." In W. N. Fenton, ed., *Symposium on Local Diversity in Iroquois Culture* (Washington: Bulletin 149, Bureau of American Ethnology).

———. 1952a. *The Modal Personality Structure of the Tuscarora Indians, as Revealed by the Rorschach Test*. Washington: Bulletin 150, Bureau of American Ethnology.

———. 1952b. "Individual Differences and Cultural Uniformities." *American Sociological Review,* 17:747-750.

———. 1956a. "Mazeway Resynthesis: A Bio-Cultural Theory of Religious Inspiration." *Transactions of the New York Academy of Sciences,* 18:626-638.

———. 1956b. "Stress and Rapid Personality Changes." *International Record of Medicine,* 169:761-774.

———. 1956c. "Revitalization Movements." *American Anthropologist,* 58:264-281.

———. 1956d. *Tornado in Worcester: An Exploratory Study of Individual and Community Behavior in an Extreme Situation*. Washington: National Academy of Sciences—National Research Council.

———. 1957. "Mazeway Disintegration: The Individual's Perception of Socio-Cultural Disorganization." *Human Organization,* 16:23-27.

———. 1958a. "Study of Processes of Organization and Revitalization of Psychological and Socio-cultural Systems. . . ." In *American Philosophical Society Yearbook, 1957*. Philadelphia: American Philosophical Society.

————. 1958b. "Dreams and the Wishes of the Soul: A Type of Psychoanalytic Theory Among the Seventeenth Century Iroquois." *American Anthropologist,* 60:234-248.

————. 1959. "Cultural Determinants of Response to Hallucinatory Experience." *A.M.A. Archives of General Psychiatry,* 1:58-69.

————. 1960a. "The Institutionalization of Cathartic and Control Strategies in Iroquois Religious Psychotherapy." In Marvin Opler, ed., *Culture and Mental Health.* (New York: Macmillan.)

————. 1960b. "The Bio-Cultural Theory of Schizophrenia." *International Record of Medicine,* 173:700-714.

————. 1961. "The Psychic Unity of Human Groups." In Bert Kaplan, ed., *Studying Personality Cross-Culturally.* Evanston: Row, Peterson.

Wallace, Anthony F. C., and Atkins, John. 1960. "The Meaning of Kinship Terms." *American Anthropologist,* 62:58-80.

Wallace, Anthony F. C., and Rashkis, H. A. 1959. "The Relation between Staff Consensus and Patient Disturbance on Mental Hospital Wards." *American Sociological Review,* 24:829-835.

Wallis, Wilson D. 1930. *Culture and Progress.* New York: McGraw-Hill.

Washburn, S. L., and Howell, F. C. 1960. "Human Evolution and Culture." In Sol Tax, ed., *The Evolution of Man* (Vol. 2 of *Evolution After Darwin*), Chicago: University of Chicago Press.

Weber, Max. 1930. *The Protestant Ethic and the Spirit of Capitalism.* New York: Scribner's.

Wechsler, David. 1930. "The Range of Human Capacities." *Scientific Monthly,* 31:35-39.

Wegrocki, Henry J. 1939. "A Critique of Cultural and Statistical Concepts of Abnormality." *Journal of Abnormal and Social Psychology*, 1939: 166-178.

White, Leslie. 1949. *The Science of Culture*. New York: Farrar, Straus.

———. 1959. "The Concept of Culture." *American Anthropologist*, 61: 227-251.

Whiting, John W. M. 1941. *Becoming a Kwoma*. New Haven: Yale University Press.

Whiting, John W. M., and Child, Irving. 1953. *Child Training and Personality*. New Haven: Yale University Press.

Whorf, Benjamin Lee. 1956. *Language, Thought, and Reality*. New York: M.I.T. Press of the Massachusetts Institute of Technology and John Wiley & Sons, Inc. Copyright, 1956, John Wiley & Sons, Inc.

Wolfenstein, Martha. 1957. *Disaster: A Psychological Essay*. Glencoe, Ill.: Free Press.

Wright, Sewall. 1931. "Evolution in Mendelian Populations." *Genetics*, 16:97-159.

This book may be kept

FOURTEEN DAYS